Life Done Right

Praise For *Life Done Right*

"'Many are called, but few are chosen'—Most people go through their entire life never realizing what their gift is and often give up when things get tough. If you want to make a significant impact, you have to stay committed through the toughest times. This is what this book is all about - keeping it real when the going get's tough!"

—Kevin Harrington
Original Shark on *Shark Tank*

"Life Done Right is an easy read with some invaluable lessons—it was hard to put this book down. I especially loved the questions for "self-reflection" at the end of each chapter, making it more than just a great story but a practical guide, where you get to learn more about yourself along the way. No matter where you are in life, this book has a lesson for you. Through the life lessons in this story, you'll be reminded that your greatest strength lies within you, and in being your true authentic self. If you have been waiting for someone to give you permission to be you, in a humble and powerful way, you've found it."

—Yolande Garrick
Personal Transformation Specialist

"There are very few books that are essential reading for anyone that wants to lead a team to world-class success. This is one of the great ones.

In this inspirational and straight-talking book, Mr. Ralph Anania reveals the secrets behind his record-breaking success. The individual story of his journey to success reveals lessons that can be applied by anyone. Whether you run a business, teach in a classroom, work in a small team or are a stay-at-home mum, this book will help you become a better leader."

—Adriana Oreskov
Business Financial Advisor

"Life Done Right has opened up a whole new world of opportunities for me. Not only has it empowered me to take control of my life again, but also become the master of my own destiny, rather than thinking it was already set in stone.

What Ralph shares in this book comes from his years of experience and straight from the heart. His methods are so simple to follow, that I find myself tapping into them on a daily basis to provide me with a clearer vision towards making better decisions, rather than getting caught up in doubt and procrastinating.

The wisdom, experiences and success that Ralph Anania shares in this book will inspire and empower you to live a purpose-filled life full of abundance."

—Donna McCoy
Food & Beverage Innovator

"The wisdom and thoughts that Ralph shares in this must-read book really make you think about your own personal experiences and how you may have let emotion get in the way of logical and constructive thinking. Ralph's understanding of Emotional Intelligence, and the way he communicates it in this easy-to-read book using his own real-life experiences, makes for a unique and clear message."

—Harry Koutsos
Director HK Advisory Group

"A lot of the mistakes I made on my road to becoming a better father to my daughter, a better man, a better partner in life and a better businessman today are all highlighted in this amazing, easy-to-read book. Hand on heart, I wish I had the opportunity to read *Life Done Right* in my early 20s while I was trying to work everything out in life.

This book would have saved me from making a lot of extremely costly mistakes, in both my personal world and also in my businesses. This book is filled with wisdom, and if you take on board and apply even half of it, it will fast-track the process, guide you to better decisions in your life and help you avoid those costly mistakes that you will risk making at some point along the way."

—Stephen Tolle
Entrepreneur & Investor

"Wow! What a brilliant read! I absolutely love this book. What makes it so incredibly special is Ralph's real, raw and authentic approach to life. He has experienced hardship and difficult experiences but has overcome them and healed himself. Ralph is the real deal and this book is truly inspiring. It makes you want to lift your game and turn your fear into faith. I respect this man immensely and refer to him as 'my hero'."

—Lina Sfetcopoulos
Managing Director

"In this simply human but deeply profound story, Ralph Anania embodies and personifies an old-world charm and grace that is sorely missing in this day and age. And with that, packs a whole lot of wisdom that is easy to digest and put into practice. The combination of being a gripping page-turner and a book that makes you want to regularly stop, reflect and be a better person, is a rare gift."

—Dev Singh
Business and Leadership Coach

LIFE DONE Right

TIMELESS WISDOM
to Give You Hope and Inspiration for the Future

RALPH ANANIA

NEW YORK

LONDON • NASHVILLE • MELBOURNE • VANCOUVER

Life Done Right

Timeless Wisdom to Give You Hope and Inspiration for the Future

© 2022 Ralph Anania

Published in New York, New York, by Morgan James Publishing. Morgan James is a trademark of Morgan James, LLC. www.MorganJamesPublishing.com

Proudly distributed by Ingram Publisher Services.

ISBN 9781631957987 paperback
ISBN 9781631957994 ebook
Library of Congress Control Number:
2021948429

Cover Design by:
Chris Treccani
www.3dogcreative.net

Interior Design by:
Christopher Kirk
www.GFSstudio.com

Morgan James is a proud partner of Habitat for Humanity Peninsula and Greater Williamsburg. Partners in building since 2006.

Get involved today! Visit MorganJamesPublishing.com/giving-back

Dedicated to...

My wonderful children
Michaela, Alexandra and Christopher

You each fill my heart with more joy than I can ever express.
As you continue to navigate through your own journey of life, I
pray
that it will be filled with an abundance of love and happiness.
And that everyone you touch, in one way or another, gets to
experience
the gift that God has given you, in shaping the world to be a
better place.

And to those that are navigating their own way through life,
remember that you have the ability to create your future
the way you want it to be,
regardless of how life looks for you right now.
Just keep moving forward and never ever give up!

I pray that in reading this book, you may find hope
and fulfilment in everything you do.

Foreword

first met Ralph when I was in my 20s. I was just starting out in business and I needed mentorship to find not only my feet as a businesswoman, but the encouragement to believe in my potential to be great.

Through just a few short interactions, Ralph touched my life deeply. Not only did he share profound advice that helped me in business—and is still with me many years later—but his presence taught me that whatever I put my heart and mind to, I can accomplish.

He has been a quiet guiding force that has shown me what I am truly capable of as a young woman, and I am deeply grateful for his love and care.

To say it has been a privilege to support Ralph to share his life and lessons with you in this book is an understatement.

Life Done Right is overflowing with valuable wisdom and principles that will guide you in creating an authentic life that has meaning and a successful business that matters. You will feel Ralph's enormous heart and the depth of his love on every page, and I know that it will be a book that you come back to time and time again when you need the encouragement to move forward in your life.

Take his wisdom into your heart and let him guide you in becoming the very best version of yourself, so that you, too, set your life up the right way.

Ralph inspires me—and I know that he will inspire you, too. Enjoy the book.

With inspiration,

Emily Gowor
Inspirational Writer & Speaker

Table of Contents

Preface

From the very first moment I put pen to paper and started writing *Life Done Right*, it was extremely important for me to open my heart and share from my own wisdom and real-life experiences. I wanted it to touch and inspire as many souls as possible and give them the comfort that no matter what storm you may be facing in your life right now, it will pass, and the sun will shine for you once again. What I wasn't quite prepared for was just how empowering the journey ahead would be, nor did I realize how much this book would evolve from the day I began writing it to the day it was published, or how much I would actually grow along with it.

There were many moments throughout the writing process that really challenged me, as I could never have imagined how deep into my memories it would take me, or how challenging it would be to dive into my innermost thoughts and feelings, or how much patience and persistence it would require for me to actually get it completed.

To say that it has required enormous effort to bring this book to life would be somewhat of an understatement. There were emotional times when I quietly shed a few tears, and at other times I struggled with it, finding myself sitting and just staring at the screen for hours. And if I'm to be completely honest, there were one or two times when I even considered giving up on it, but I couldn't; the vision I saw of how this book could impact your life was far too alluring and important for me to walk away from. My mission in life is to inspire and to make a real difference in someone else's life, and none more so than our next generation, and that motivation is what kept me focused to ensure I delivered what I set out to achieve.

And so, without compromise, I continued to push through every challenge I encountered until it reached this very moment where you are holding this book firmly in your hands. Hand on heart, I can say that every single hour spent placing words where they belong and every moment where I pushed through to deliver this book to you has been well and truly worth it.

To me, *Life Done Right* is not just a book; it is an expression of my purpose. My greatest wish and highest hope while writing it was that it will help you to find and fulfil your own purpose, too. I hope that the value you gain from it touches you enough to really usher in the understanding of how to connect your calling, your purpose and your heart in a way that will inspire you to go out and make a difference to the human race.

You will find, in these pages, my heart as well as the deepest wisdom I have gained on how to make your life one that is truly worth living. As you embark on the journey of reading this book, it is my heartfelt wish that I have achieved my mission and that, by the time you turn the last page, you will know what your heart truly yearns to do and have the courage to pursue it without hesitation, regardless of how that looks or where it takes you.

I pray that each page will help you to see greater possibilities for yourself so that you can experience what I believe is the most inspiring way to live and work: from your soul. May you find the answers you have been seeking about the greater meaning of your life.

And may you catch a lasting glimpse of how magnificent you are, so that you never give up on the journey of fulfilling the inspiring destiny you were placed on the earth for.

Life is a notebook. Two pages are already written by God, the first page is birth and the last page is death, and the center pages are for you to fill with all the memories you create in between.

Ralph Anania

Introduction

T ime. That space between sowing a seed and reaping the rewards, between planning and execution, between promise and fulfilment. We live in such a fast-moving world where everything has become 'click and collect', where everyone has become accustomed to instant gratification, where the concept of having to wait can be quite frustrating for many. Yet, when we understand our true purpose and how we can play our part in making a real difference in the world, we start to align ourselves with what God really put us on this earth to achieve.

Life is a wonderful gift and, for many, never truly appreciated until they're faced with some form of adversity. At some point in our lives, we are all going to experience adversity, be it the tragedy of losing a friend or family member, the breakdown of a marriage or relationship, financial ruin or a business collapse.

Whatever that is, the most important takeaway for me were the lessons I *needed* to learn. Most of us rely on our ego to get us through day by day, and while ego is not always a bad thing, it's not where you want to *live* 24/7. You need to be aware of what is happening around you. Ego will protect you in certain situations, but will destroy you if you hold on to it all the time.

The challenge for most of us is that we have become so conditioned to certain things or certain ways that we don't even realize it. What we feed will grow; water doesn't know the difference between a plant and a weed, and the same applies to energy. If you're putting all your energy into feeding your ego, then that's what will grow. This is where awareness comes into play. You need to be aware when this starts to occur and decide if this is where you want to put all your energy into, and 'how' it will serve you if you do.

Each and every one of us is born with a gift. A select few realize their gift early in life, but then there are others who live their entire life feeling lost and never finding what their gift really is. One of my favorite verses from the greatest book of all time is found in Matthew 22:14, "For many are called, but few are chosen." The reality is that we are ALL called, every single person on the planet is born with a purpose which is our gift, and the reason 'few are chosen' is that society has taught us to 'give up' too easily, never allowing us to figure out what our true purpose really is.

My purpose in writing this book is to share my journey, my real-life experiences, and inspire you to sit back, reflect and identify or acknowledge where some of the shortfalls are appearing in your life. If we're to be completely honest and take a good hard look at ourselves in the mirror, we can notice many areas in our life that we can change or make adjustments to, before it's too late.

You see, the markers are always there; we just choose to ignore them, and when they hit us right smack in the middle of the forehead, we don't even realize what has just happened. In the blink of an eye, your world can be turned upside down and inside out, and for some stupid reason you can't even understand why.

The one thing that I can say is that once you do understand and accept the lesson behind what has happened, you come to a place where everything starts to become crystal clear. You see things that you never saw before, what you thought mattered in the past no longer does, and you start to understand what your true purpose in life really is. From the lessons learnt, you get a second chance to create your future the way you want it to be.

COVID-19 has changed the world as we knew it forever. No one was prepared for this. Besides, the media has done such an amazing job of instilling fear into everyone, that not only did it cause panic like we've never seen before but it also brought global economies to their knees. Unfortunately, for the majority of society, it takes something like this to understand and appreciate what they have and how they've taken some of the most important things in life for granted.

I've always had a never-give-up attitude, which has shaped me into being an extremely high achiever. That said, when you're at the top of your game, you can get extremely lonely if you let it get to you. And as a leader, when you have many people relying on you, you can fall into a trap of believing that you have to take on or fix everyone else's issues, often forgetting or disregarding the needs of those closest to you.

A lot has been written over the years on the topic of work-life balance, but the reality is that there is just life. We're all on this planet for a 'reason' and a 'season' and for some, that season is longer than for others. The challenge most people have is navigating through it without causing too much damage, and by that I mean finding the time to take care of yourself first and then those closest to you. Life is a journey which is governed by the choices we make on a daily basis. When you can keep yourself in check and follow through with discipline, the obstacles that will undoubtedly appear every so often will be much easier to deal with.

It took a long time for me to get to the point of understanding that, and while today I can say that I have mastered the art, it didn't come easy. There were many lessons and a lot of pain along the way. I will share more on that as we move on.

What happens, though, is that we tend to become consumed in our own success. While success is different for everyone, because we live in a very material driven world where it's all about the possessions we accumulate, we tend to measure one's 'success' by what they have 'accumulated.' The truth is that success without happiness is failure. The world is full of very 'successful' people who have NEVER experienced happiness. So regardless of what point you've reached in your life, it's never too late to change. If nothing else, I hope this book can open your eyes and give you an inspiring vision to the opportunities that are there waiting for you.

Fulfilling a purpose greater than your own self by serving others is the greatest gift. Stay grounded and humble and don`t ever see those qualities as signs of weakness.

RALPH ANANIA

Chapter 1:

From Humble Beginnings

I was born and raised in Western Sydney. My parents left Italy during a very tough economic era and migrated to Australia in the early 1960s to find a better life for their young family. If you were to go back in history, you will find that Italian families who migrated to Australia during the 1940s, 1950s, 1960s and even 1970s carried with them very strong family principles.

This was no different for my parents. Family was everything to them, and giving their children every opportunity for a better life than the one they had left behind in Italy was their topmost priority. That strong family connection that I was raised in is something that I have carried through to my own family, which is why, today, my children are my entire world.

Growing up in the late 1960s and 1970s as the child of an immigrant family wasn't easy. My parents owned the local 'fruit shop', and I went to school and lived in the same suburb. While I was born in Australia, I was still the child of Italian parents, and therefore I was labelled a 'wog'—a term that still makes me cringe whenever I hear it. In those days, being a 'wog' also came with an enormous amount of bullying, and the only difference was that back then, no one even knew what bullying was.

There wasn't a great deal you could do about it, because even the teachers at school were very racist, so the choice was to either put up with it or retaliate. The problem with retaliating, however, was that the few times I dealt with the kid who was bullying me, not only did I get in trouble at school (to which punishment in those days was the CANE, yep, hands out and six across each hand) but I also copped the belt across my buttocks when I got home for getting in trouble at school. Needless to say, I did not enjoy school at all. When I look back now and reflect, it really saddens me, because there were a number of subjects that I really enjoyed and had there been just a small amount of support, I may have had a very different experience.

What happens in life though is that we tend to take on and own what has been instilled in us from a very young age and, whether good, bad or indifferent, we go through life carrying a certain amount of baggage that we've inherited without us even realizing it. That in itself plays a huge part in how you live out your life, and the actions and consequences surrounding you are a direct reflection of all the heavy baggage that you continue to carry around with you.

Unfortunately, some of life's greatest lessons that come from our parents are not realized until after they're gone. I spent much of my childhood alongside my father, predominantly in and around the family business, and this is where most of my entre-preneurial lessons came from. It started off when Dad began taking me with him to visit the local farmers and pick up the fresh produce directly from the farm, and then extended to the 3 a.m. drive to the Central Wholesale Markets, which in those days were located in Haymarket, Sydney. If my memory serves me correctly, I was around four years old then.

There was a lot of activity and a great atmosphere in those days, both at the farms and the markets, and I absolutely loved the excitement and the incredible hustle and bustle of it all. Watching my father pull out his pocket-knife and cut the fruit to make sure it was good enough for his customers, and then negotiate the best price with the suppliers, was where I learnt the 'art of negotiation.'

My dad would deal with farmers from all over the country who would bring their own produce into the central markets to sell. He knew a lot of them from his childhood days back in Italy, which made for great conversations on the hour-long drive back home. Some of those stories had incredible lessons in them, which have served me well over the years.

Dad would explain the relationships he had with everyone and how respect had to be earned and how your integrity was never negotiable. The conversation would then shift to explaining why he had purchased a large quantity of a particular product that day, as it was the peak of the season and he was able to negotiate a great price, so his customers could take advantage of it. He used to say that he had a 'present' for his customers, as he was able to lower the selling price because of his amazing negotiation skills with the suppliers.

Mastering the art of selling and delivering exceptional customer service was also something I learnt from my father. My dad knew his business because he knew what his customers wanted. In those days, cool rooms and cold storage facilities were a rarity, and therefore, you had to get back to your store early enough to ensure you sold all that you purchased at the central market that day; otherwise, the produce would spoil and have to be thrown out.

Dad would always be walking around the store with his pocket-knife out, cutting fruit and letting his customers try a piece before they made any purchase. You would be amazed at the difference this would make, when selling something that tasted really sweet and fantastic, the customers would automatically buy more because they knew that when they took that product home it would get eaten and not be wasted. This is how Dad kept growing his business, and I used the same fundamentals many years later in growing a $130M empire.

The flipside, however, was that my dad never came to a single sporting event of mine, and things like parent-teacher interviews only occurred when I got in trouble and Dad was asked to come and meet with the principal, which was never a pretty experience. Let's just say that my father had a very persuasive way of making the principal see things his way, and in turn the principal was always very apologetic for wasting my father's time.

My mother, on the other hand, was one of the strongest women I have ever known. She went through a very tough childhood, being the eldest child and losing her father at a very young age. Growing up in the years that followed the Great Depression compelled her to take on the role of looking after her siblings, so her mother could go to work and put food on the table. This meant that she could no longer go to school and only got as far as the equivalent of Grade 3.

Not long after my parents were married, my father was shipped off to serve in the military where he did his compulsory years of service. Work was hard to come by and in 1960, he left Italy for his long journey to Australia in search of a better life for his family. Upon arrival, Dad had no issue finding work, doing 18-hour days, seven days a week.

He worked as a concreter on the construction of the famous Warragamba Dam for the first half of the day, and then worked the afternoons/evenings and weekends in one of his friend's fruit shops, where he would carve his craft as an exceptional fresh produce retailer. Two years later, he had saved enough money for the trip to bring Mum, my oldest brother Joe and older sisters Lucy and Anna across to Australia, where they got to settle as a family again and start a new life together. I then came along in 1964 and my younger brother Frank in 1968, and the family was complete.

A few years later, Dad went on to open his own fruit shop. Mum and my older brother Joe would get up in the early hours of the morning to go and get the store ready for the day's trading, while Dad was at the markets purchasing the required produce to bring back for his customers. Meanwhile at home, everyone knew their place and what they had to do. One of the things that was drilled into me as a kid was that first thing to do when I got up in the morning was to make my bed, which, believe it or not, instils such a huge amount of discipline. This was followed by immaculate grooming, which is why I have such attention to detail. God forbid should we attempt to go out the door and not have clean and ironed clothes or clean polished shoes on! That said, it is a wonderful trait that I am forever grateful to my mother for.

The unconditional love my mother had for her children, and later in life for her grandchildren, was incredible—another of those things you don't realize you've gained until they're gone. My mother showed her love most through her cooking; no matter what time of the day it was, if you showed up and she knew you hadn't eaten, she would cook up a feast in no time. There were no recipes or measuring cups, it was all done through her wisdom and insights. Many years later I would realize that those same insights flowed through to me.

Some of the best meals I have cooked were at times when I could swear my mother was right beside me, because I had no idea what I was doing, yet it all came together with unbelievable ease. She carried an enormous amount of pain through her entire life, yet you would never know, and her wisdom was incredible and something I will cherish forever.

Those life lessons have kept me grounded and have molded me into the person I am today. I will never forget the years of early morning trips to the central markets or the value of building great relationships or making my bed as soon as I get up each morning, which I still do to this day.

One should always remember and cherish those real-life lessons and humble beginnings. I've seen many people over the years who have achieved 'financial' success who forget where they started or are ashamed of what their background is, which is very sad. The arrogance they have developed as a result keeps them from passing anything of emotional value on to their own children, who then have little or no respect for their heritage and culture and think that they are better than everyone else because they have the money to flaunt and are 'entitled.'

The lessons you learn in life should never limit you from achieving greatness, no matter how that looks for you. What is important to remember though is that the restriction on what you can achieve will only come from the limiting beliefs you put on yourself. If your goal is to achieve greatness, then that's where your focus must be. Remember, what you feed will grow. If you allow your limiting beliefs to consume you, then that's where you'll stop, but if you put your energy into creating great outcomes, you will continue to grow. The choice is entirely yours.

You should always be grateful for what you have and where you've come from, regardless of what that little voice in your head is telling you. When I look back at my life, I could quite easily blame my parents for not getting involved in my schoolwork, or not coming to my sports games, along with a million other silly meaningless things.

The reality is that times were different then, and they had their own struggles in addition to the challenge of running a business in a country where they barely knew the language. Their focus was to give us, their children, a better shot at life. I wouldn't be the person I am today, nor would I have achieved half of what I have achieved, if it wasn't for what I was able to learn from my parents.

Being grateful for what you have is the first step to achieving success. And there's the old saying: When life hands you lemons, go and make lemonade. The problem is that most people tend to focus on how sour the lemons are, rather than expanding their mind to create something good out of what they've been given. The 'poor me' syndrome never serves anyone, so regardless of where you are or what you're going through, if you're determined to look for the positive in every situation, you'll find solutions without even realizing it.

Your Life In Reflection

- Some of the greatest lessons we learn in life come from our parents, but unfortunately, sometimes they are not realized until long after our parents are gone. What lessons have you taken from your parents that you can appreciate and thank them for right now?
- What areas do you need to look at in your life, which have limited you from achieving greatness, regardless of how that looks for you?
- Being grateful is the first step to achieving success. What are you truly grateful for?

Success requires full payment upfront! Those who succeed do so because they are committed to an outcome and are prepared to persist and persevere regardless of what obstacles are put before them.

RALPH ANANIA

Chapter 2:
Define Your Own Success

S uccess is different for everyone. From my own experiences in dealing with hundreds of business leaders large and small, most people think that being successful means having a lot of money. However, success is not measured by the amount of money you have or what possessions you have accumulated. Rather, success is measured by what you have been able to achieve and contribute to making a difference in the world and how many lives you've impacted as a result.

I will say this though: Success is balance. When you have the right balance in your life and everything is flowing evenly—that is, your business or work life is under control, your family life is fulfilled and taken care of, and you have enough time out for yourself—then and only then will you experience real success, because success without happiness is superficial.

For me, without an inkling of doubt, success is in seeing my children grow and evolve into the amazing young adults they've become today, and when I sit back and reflect on their journey and what each of them has achieved thus far, I feel great pride and a sense of accomplishment. That, for me, is priceless.

As a parent, it's our responsibility to ensure we give our children every opportunity to become the change we want to see in the world, because they are our future. Today, more than ever before, we need to support, guide and inspire them and not just provide for them. I know many parents who have given their children everything except their time, only for them to end up being complete disasters and causing their families a lifetime of grief.

Your children need *you*, not just your money. You need to teach them what is required for them to enjoy the luxuries you provide for them, and have them appreciate it all and not just expect it to be given freely because you're their parent.

I have a beautiful framed saying that reads:

A hundred years from now, it would not have mattered what size your bank account was, what sort of house you lived in, or the kind of car you drove, but the world may be different because of the role you played in the life of your children.

This has had a spot on my desk for over 20 years. I look at it every single day to never forget the importance of the role I play in the life of my children.

Social media has done a great job of acclimatizing society to living in a very materialistic world, which has definitely changed the way we live life today. In many ways, we seem to have lost appreciation for the sacrifices our parents and grandparents made for us to be where we are now. It has saddened me greatly to see the entire world go through the COVID-19 pandemic. So many lives have been lost because of this horrid infectious disease. I truly believe this has also been one of the greatest reality checks of modern times. The mere fact that we have had to isolate at home and spend time with one another and communicate and connect in a way that doesn't require any electronic device has been one of the best things that could have happened. It has taken us back to a time when life was a lot simpler and everyone was much healthier and happier.

Everyone has realized that the simple things in life we take for granted on a daily basis matter the most. Life is not about the big houses, sports cars, private jets or yachts, it's about connecting with one another and working towards a greater good. I'm not saying that you can't or shouldn't have nice things; absolutely you can and should have them if you can afford them. But don't let those 'things' make you think that you are better than someone else, as material possessions do not define success.

What you see as success certainly changes as you get older. I too went through a phase in my life where I based success on what I had accumulated and could afford to buy as opposed to what difference I was making and contributing in the life of someone else. Reaching that point, where you have everything but happiness, is when you understand the real meaning of success. We are all born with a purpose, but sadly some of us never get to realize what that purpose is because we're so caught up in our own importance that we miss our calling completely. But when you live your life through the purpose that you were called for, success happens without you even noticing, because your focus is no longer on becoming successful, it's on living your true purpose.

I have been with many senior executives and business leaders over the years who would manage to put up a great façade. Unfortunately for them, I could pick it up a mile away, so when I called them out on it, after their initial shock, they would open up and confess how they felt like a total fraud. Now, they're not a fraud at all, but they wrongly assume they are because they have allowed themselves to get drawn into a fake world, always worrying about the need to impress, rather than stepping up, being a leader, inspiring others and making a real difference, which brings me back to purpose.

I fell in this trap myself over the years, and let me tell you, it is a horrible place to be. You go through every day believing you need to impress others to uphold an image that you created without even realizing it. This is dangerous ground that breeds uncertainty, resulting in making wrong decisions that have consequences attached to them.

One thing I want to make very clear to you is, don't ever become consumed about 'looking good' to impress. It doesn't matter, and the truth is that no one even cares. What I've come to realize over the years is that the people who are out to impress the most are the ones who harbor serious personal issues that they're hiding or running from.

Authenticity is real; everyone around you can feel it and see it clearly, just as they can see when someone is putting on a mask and being fake, trying hard to be someone they're not. Authenticity is doing the right thing, being who you really are naturally. When you are true to yourself and everything about you is real, you will stand out like a bright shiny star that everyone can see without any effort.

I'm known for making a real difference in many people's lives, getting them to realize what life is really about, how to create balance and not get caught up in the nonsense that society dishes out to all of us every single day.

I didn't go to university, nor was I an A-grade student, but I had a passion for business and became an entrepreneur at a very young age. I learnt a lot from my father, which is why it is very important for me to be the best father to my children and give them the guidance and wisdom that will help them evolve into the best version of themselves that they can be, whatever that looks like. All three of my children are very different in character; however, they hold the same passion as I do in becoming the best they can at whatever they put their mind to.

I have supported and will continue to support each of them on their own journey. Regardless of what they achieve, as long as they are living their purpose, they are well on their way to achieving their own version of the success they deserve.

Your Life In Reflection

- Success is not measured by how much money you have or what possessions you have accumulated. Success is measured by what you have been able to achieve and contribute to making a difference in the world and how many lives you've been able to change as a result.
- How do you currently measure success?
- What does success mean to you?

The promises you keep will determine your future. Once you commit to the promises you make to yourself, there is nothing that can hold you back.

RALPH ANANIA

Chapter 3:
Know Your Core Values & Live By Them

Core values are developed and defined in response to what you've experienced throughout your journey of life. What you believe to be true may not necessarily be someone else's truth. Sadly, a vast majority of people don't even know what their core values are.

My core values have not only changed but have also evolved as I've become older and experienced the many challenges thrown at me along the way. Depending on your upbringing, there are certain values that are instilled in you as a child that stay with you forever, because you believe them strongly enough that you continue to live by them even as you grow older.

I was raised in a Christian family and my faith is something that I value deeply from my childhood, as God has played a huge part in my life. For me, saying grace at the dinner table and giving thanks for our food and our day is extremely important.

There are millions of people around the world who don't have food every night, let alone the privilege to even sit at the dinner table, so I am absolutely grateful for that.

With that also come certain conditions, one of them being no mobile phones at the dinner table, because if nothing else, that little time we get to spend together as a family while having dinner is when we enjoy a conversation, a laugh and at times even some banter. There have been many laughs and many memories associated with the discussions we've had at the dinner table. And while my children may not realize the preciousness of that today, they most certainly will when they are sitting and having dinner with their own children someday, maybe even sharing one of my dad jokes that they've come to love and appreciate, even though they like to pretend they don't.

I value my time at the dinner table with my children more than ever, as we quite often get caught up with life. And while it wasn't always like that for me, the time you spend at the dinner table with your family is where some of life's most valuable lessons will likely come from. A discussion at the dinner table could lead you to expressing your views, allow you to share your past experiences and also explain why you hold certain views that could eventually morph and become your core values.

So, as I sit here today, one of my core values is definitely having dinner together as a family. Now I'm aware that as the children get older, this will become even more of a challenge, because there will be other commitments, be it training, college, work, boyfriends or girlfriends. Getting everyone together isn't always easy, but even if it's just a couple of nights per week, it still carries that same level of importance.

My father migrated to Australia with nothing more than a suitcase, made huge sacrifices and worked hard for everything he had. I am forever grateful for the time we spent together when I was young and the lessons he taught me, which, at the time, I had no idea would play such an important part in my life. Among the many lessons, there were two things that he was really big on: respect and integrity.

He would always say that respect is something you have to earn, and if you want to be respected you need to show respect first. And your integrity is something that you should never have questioned, meaning that you always do the right thing regardless of any external influence; otherwise, it would always find its way back and haunt you. To this day, respect and integrity are at the center of my core values.

You'll know what your core values are once you truly start to believe and live by what really matters to you. When you are aligned with what you believe and what you live by, you set the standards that are exhibited to the external world and what everyone else sees. I have personally mentored and coached thousands of people in 14 different countries across the globe in a wide range of cultures and upbringings, and I have seen many people trying to be someone they're not and living someone else's life.

The main reason for this is that they simply have no idea of what their core values are and have been caught up in the materialistic idea of having to 'look' a certain way to gain any sort of attention. This is a very shallow and superficial way of living, where you have no connection to your spiritual self. This will, more often than not, lead to a long dark road of depression because you have no idea what your purpose in life is.

The universe has a way of correcting itself and if there's one good thing that has come out of the COVID-19 pandemic, it's that everyone has been forced to stop and reflect on what life is really about. And while it's had such a deep impact on everyone—some more than others with the tragic loss of a loved one—it has opened our eyes to what really is and isn't important in life. This in itself has created a shift, allowing us to reset, realign and refocus on what we really value in life and the changes we would like to bring moving forward.

Life is not about setting standards that require you to act a certain way; rather, the standards you set for yourself must come from within, reflecting what you truly believe and value, not what some Facebook or Instagram post tells you to be. While social media has helped in bringing people together and sharing what is happening in their life, it has also created a dark side where people are believing everything that is posted.

This starts to create insecurity, because you have allowed yourself to 'believe' what is being posted is true and that you're missing out, telling yourself that you're not good enough or worthy enough. Worse, all this is based off other insecure people wanting the world to believe they are living this great life. So not only are you getting drawn into their 'fake' world, but it also doesn't serve you, and before you know it you've allowed yourself to spiral into a depressive state. When you take the time and do the personal work to find out who you really are, **EVERYTHING** changes, and if you look at what really serves you and what doesn't in life, you will start to find your core values.

If you've ever found yourself wondering *why* you do certain things that you do, a great resource to study are the six human needs. These will give you some clarity around what drives certain behaviors that you've taken on over the long term. To help you gain some clarity for now, here's a little explanation for each one, but there is a lot more you can research yourself if you want to go deeper.

1. Certainty
    This is our need to be free from any form of worry or anxiety. To get to this point, we need to develop a certain amount of consistency, so we don't have to worry about anything in a particular area. An example could be owning a house, so you never have to worry about not having a roof over your head.

2. Uncertainty/Variety
    Some people are quite spontaneous and like to do things without too much thought, because they crave variety. If you ask these people why they're like that, they will tell you that life would be boring without variety.

3. Significance
    This is the need to feel special, because people want to be noticed. Some people gain significance from covering their body with tattoos or piercings, some get it from making a lot of money and having all the toys that come with it. It's different for everyone, which again depends on what they believe is their core value.

4. Connection/Love

   This is where we like to feel that we belong, that we're not alone, not just in a physical sense but also from a mental state. There are a lot of people who feel lonely inside their head, which then drives them to depression, when in fact they are actually adored and loved by everyone they connect with.

5. Growth

   Let's face it, we're either growing or dying. Growth brings happiness as there is a certain element of achievement and satisfaction that comes with it. It's how we evolve.

6. Contribution

   This is where we leave this world having made a difference. It's one of the greatest areas of fulfilment when you can make a positive difference in someone else's life.

Whether you're consciously aware of it or not, your top four needs are being met every single day and by default have become crucial to your survival. What makes this a bit more interesting it that everyone prioritizes them differently depending on what's happening in their life. The reason I say that these needs are being met, whether you're aware of it or not, is that over time these have developed into a habit, because you've subconsciously chosen how to be, act or live your life in these domains.

One of the most relevant examples of this can be seen in people who have found 'fame', who have unconsciously made 'significance' their number one need. What happens quite often, though, is that we see these people spiral out of control, because they don't know what their core values are. Despite having all the money and material things, they don't have the love or connection that brings happiness, so they turn to drugs and alcohol to try and find it.

I'm not saying that you can't have some of the nicer things that money can buy; I'm saying that having them without understanding your core values is meaningless. Two of the six needs that come from your core are growth and contribution, because by helping someone else you not only grow as a person, but also achieve a sense of euphoria in your spiritual being, an area that most of society have zero connection to.

While this may seem somewhat overwhelming to take on, the most important part of this process is to just let go of all your limiting beliefs and bring yourself to a state of just being present. Let go of all the thoughts that don't serve you and learn to be in the moment, for that's the starting point to setting 'standards' for yourself and your life. Now, be very mindful that you don't mistake standards for rules, because they are very different. A rule is what someone else has told you to follow, something you *should* do. There is so much more that you can learn in this area and I encourage you to explore it fully. With time, you will start to understand more about yourself, which is undoubtedly great for you but also for those closest to you.

Your Life In Reflection

- When you take the time and do the personal work to find out who you really are, everything changes, and if you look at what serves you and what doesn't in life, you will start to find your core values. What personal work do you need to do on yourself to find what your core values are for you?

- Once you start to believe and live by what really matters to you, you'll come to truly know what your core values are. How does that reflect on you? What are those core values for you?

One thing we all have equally is time.
Life is too short, don't waste time
making excuses, spend your time
making every second count.

RALPH ANANIA

Chapter 4:
Don't Waste Your Time

Time is one thing we all have equally, but as a society we tend to be very wasteful of it. We all have 24 hours in a day, and if we're to get the best use out of those hours, we need to be disciplined and resourceful and not waste the time we have. People often say, "I'll get to it tomorrow," but the same thing will keep happening every day; they'll keep saying they'll get to it tomorrow, but tomorrow will never come if they don't do it today. The best way to get the most out of every 24 hours is to put structure in your day, week and month, which requires discipline.

Most people don't value their time. When I say this, I'm not speaking from a financial perspective but from a resource perspective. At some point in our lives, we have all been guilty of not valuing the time that we have and just taking it for granted. Unfortunately for most, we only come to truly understand the real value of time when we (or a loved one) are diagnosed with a terminal illness. This is when the wakeup call hits home and we suddenly realize the value of time now that there's a limit on it. We go through life thinking we're invincible, and it's not until we get a wakeup call that we realize we're not.

What I have come to learn and appreciate is that our time here on earth is limited. It amazes me how most people tend to be content living someone else's life, not even realizing this. What I mean by this is that they have a job they don't particularly enjoy, but they still do it because they've gone through the traditional upbringing of going to school and being taught they need to get good grades so that they can go out and get a good job.

The problem with that is, more times than not, they end up in a job or a career that they don't really enjoy, and they tend to stay in it just because it pays the bills, they've been there for a long time and have created a certain lifestyle that they've become accustomed to. In other words, they have basically become complacent without even realizing it. It's like being a hamster on a wheel. They do the same thing day in and day out, just killing time and looking forward to the day they retire. While this may seem like I'm generalizing and I can understand why you may think that, just take a minute and look at the people you know and how they are or have been living their lives. When you examine that scenario a little more, you will see clearly that what I'm saying is actually happening to more people than you originally thought.

The reality is that the day of retirement is the day they're being walked down the aisle in a box. We should be utilizing our time while we're on earth living and breathing, without letting retirement come into it. I think the word 'retirement' to a lot of people just signals an 'end'—end to life, in many ways, because they switch off mentally as well as physically. So many people who retire are gone within a couple of years.

This is particularly the case when someone has had no hobbies or interests outside of work. They're gone because what has kept them going is lost; they've basically shut down. This is the way society conditions us. Time is just as precious as the air we breathe, but because we've been conditioned to live in a material world, we don't put a physical value on time, just as we don't put a physical value on the air we breathe. We don't think of it that way, but if someone was to hold your head under water until you couldn't get up, you'd appreciate how valuable air is. It's the same with time. We just take it for granted. However, the time we lose today is gone forever and we'll never get that back; we *can't* get that back. This makes it even more important to reassess where you're at and to live life with purpose, so that you can have no regrets.

Over the years, I have come to identify three areas where change was required to ensure I made the most of my time.

First: Look at areas in your life where you've been putting things off. Where have you procrastinated, or where have you kept putting things on the back burner? Whenever you find yourself putting things off, it's actually depleting or even stealing your time, but what's worse is it's also stealing your success because you're not able to achieve what you want to achieve. Valuing the time that you have will help prevent putting things off, allowing you to then be more proactive.

One of the best tools I've become disciplined to use throughout my career is a calendar. I use a calendar religiously, and everything I do has a time allocated to it. My clients and anyone I work with will have access to my calendar, and they can book in a time for themselves. I do it this way for two reasons: one, my availability is crystal clear on the calendar, and the times I need for personal or other matters are already blocked out so there can be no clash; and two, having everyone utilise my calendars (I have different time slots for different people) allows me to make the most out of my day. Even if I've had a 12-hour day, it has been 12 full hours of progress, not a 12-hour day in which I've only done four hours of productive work because I've fluffed around doing things that are not important.

Second: To make the most out of time, you need to learn how to be productive. Putting a value on time not only helps you become more productive but also more effective, enabling you to achieve your goals. Most people who set goals neither set a timeline nor hold themselves accountable, and therefore they don't achieve them. When you set goals and have a timeline *and* you value time, those goals get achieved, allowing you to move forward and reap the rewards, which in most people's eyes is called success. Success, as I've said before, is different for everybody, so the achievement of any goal is success, regardless of how big or small it is.

By learning to be productive, you also learn to do things smarter. This ensures you're not wasting time and you're able to make better decisions, which ultimately gives you more control of your life because you're able to achieve greater results. Once you've got all this in order, it takes away a ton of stress because you're no longer rushing to get things done or having last-minute panic attacks over needing to fill a schedule or running out of time.

From my own experience, successful people learn to control their own time to achieve the success they deserve. This is one of the main distinguishing characteristics of successful people. They don't waste time, because for them, time is as valuable as money.

Third: When you learn the real value of time, it will allow you to look at how time affects your health and wellbeing. We all need downtime, time to relax and unwind, and quality time with our family and loved ones. This time should be non-negotiable, and when it's a priority, it will elevate you in so many different aspects of your life. Valuing the time that you have with your family is very important.

Speaking from experience, there are far too many people who work 18 hours a day, six or seven days a week. While I can appreciate there may be challenging times or circumstances that make us believe we need to work those hours to achieve a result or to keep going, this is only a limiting belief that we hold. It's a belief that doesn't serve you. There was a point in my life where I worked seven days a week for seven years straight; I didn't have a holiday for seven years. It was one of those periods in my life when I had experienced some financial difficulties through the business and I just kept pushing through to continue to build and grow. Looking back today, it was not a smart move.

What happens is that you become less productive, you become frustrated, *and* you become irritable with those around you. I've been there in the past and trust me when I say that this is not a good place to be. I know that life in general can be very busy, I get it, but if we fail to value time, we generally end up wasting it on unnecessary things. This can adversely affect your relationships, especially with the ones you love most, be it your spouse, partner, or children.

So, learning to value and manage your time, and getting to a point where you can do it extremely well, will lead to a significant drop in stress levels and a much better chance of improving your overall health. In short, you'll be living a much happier life.

What the next chapter in your life looks like will ultimately be determined by the value of your time. Time is too short to waste, especially when it's being wasted on destiny destroyers, these are things that drain you from achieving your goals. So whatever you give time to in the next chapter, make it worthwhile. Don't waste it.

How many people waste their time trying to go back to yesterday, hanging on to past baggage, even when it doesn't serve them? Far too many. If you're driving along the road and continually looking in the rear-view mirror, at some point you're going to have an accident. Focus on looking forward and forget about the past because you can't change it. You can only navigate through the time you have now, creating your future the way you want it to be.

There's a song by Reba McEntire called *If I had Only Known,* which explains the value of time perfectly. If you haven't heard it, listen to the lyrics and you'll understand what I mean.

Your Life In Reflection

- The best way to get the most out of every 24 hours is to put structure in your day, week and month, which requires discipline.
- Time is just as precious as the air we breathe, but because we've been conditioned to live in a material world, we don't put a physical value on time, just as we don't put a physical value on the air we breathe. How well do you manage your time and what value do you put on it?

*The most powerful source of opportunity is found through collaboration and partnership. When the two align,
magical things start to manifest.*

RALPH ANANIA

Chapter 5:

Nurture Your Relationships

Something that I believe has been regrettably lost in today's modern world is the real value of human interaction and connection. That said, the universe has a wonderful way of showing us that some adjustments must be made, and COVID-19 has done just that. While the forced isolation period in lockdown was tough on some, it was life-changing for others. What this did was bring back valuable family time and keep all external distractions away, letting us all create valuable memories—something that unfortunately has been lost for most of society.

Technology has come a long way in the past 20 years and for many of us, fully immersed like we are in the digital age, it's hard to imagine a world before the internet or smartphones existed. But while technology has made our lives more convenient, there's also the negative aspect which has had an effect on our communication skills.

Just as technology has allowed us to be more efficient with our time, I believe it has also, in a lot of ways, made us somewhat lazy. Why? Because it's too easy to send a text message instead of dialing the number and having a real conversation, and over time, this starts to have a huge impact on the way we communicate. Just watch a group of teens sitting together, and you'll likely notice that each one of them is on their phone texting instead of having a conversation.

We see kids lock themselves away in their room playing video games all day instead of getting outside, being physically active and taking in the nourishment and goodness of mother nature. Our bodies need sunlight; the number of people who are vitamin D deficient is incredible. We then have the other issues that come with kids being glued to a screen all day: behavioral issues, obesity, sleeping disorders and in some cases even violence.

This then morphs into higher levels of stress, which creates more illnesses, which then drives more prescription drugs, which then pushes so many people into depression. Mental illness is a bigger problem in society today than it has ever been in the history of mankind. The need of the hour is to maintain some level of balance. Technology has allowed us to do more, achieve more and create more than ever before, but finding the right balance has to come from discipline, which is also about responsibility. I appreciate the challenges and stress that parents face in today's world, and it can be easier at times to give a child an iPad or a smartphone to keep them entertained, but this needs to be in moderation. Sadly, most people use technology to keep their children entertained every waking minute, which is where the real underlying problem begins.

That said, technology has become a significant part of our lives and I believe it has more positive benefits than negative. Knowing what the possible negative effects can be on certain aspects of life will help us find ways to minimize them, so we can still enjoy all the positive aspects that technology continues to deliver.

While technology has allowed us to reach more people and converse more often, we need to take that and use it as an opportunity to connect at a deeper level. I have had the privilege of working with some amazing clients over the years, some of whom have become very close friends. I remember going to an event back in 2010 when I first moved into the coaching/mentoring space. One of the speakers there was selling his course on 'How To Build A Coaching Business' and made a comment that stuck with me for some reason.

They said that in the coaching space, the lifecycle of a client was between 6 and 12 months and very rarely would they exceed 18 months. I remember thinking, *wow, this is quite different to what I have experienced in the past*, but fast forward ten years to 2020 and nearly all of my private one-on-one clients that I've had the privilege of working with have been with me for 3–4 years and have achieved some incredible results, not only in their business but more importantly in their personal life.

There may be a few reasons why this is the case, but the standout is that I take the time to build a rapport, really getting to understand what's going on for them, digging deeper and deeper until we get to the core and then working our way through step by step. There are a lot of people out there who have the title of a 'business coach' but have never owned a business and have never experienced the challenges that come with owning a business. These coaches give vanilla cookie-cutter textbook advice on a situation that they know nothing about, and the poor client doesn't know any different so they take that advice on board, only to learn a few months down the track that it was the wrong advice and consequently end up in a deep hole.

Meanwhile, the self-proclaimed business coach has moved on, because they've seen the writing on the wall leaving this poor individual in a serious predicament. I acknowledge that this *may* be generalizing it, but I've seen this play out first-hand with numerous business owners who have come up to me at events and shared their story in tears, devastated and totally broken because of the wrong advice given by someone who hasn't taken the time upfront to understand what's driving them and their business.

Building relationships takes time, and it needs trust, which doesn't happen in a 30-minute 'discovery' call; it happens by investing the time upfront and getting to know where their challenges are and what's driving them and their business. For most entrepreneurs, their business is their life and in a lot of cases, they don't know how to separate the two. This in itself is not the problem, but it is crucial to understanding on a deeper level what actually drives them to do what they do and what their aspirations are.

I have honestly lost count of the times I've been called to meet with a potential client who wanted help with their business and the entire conversation was about them and what was driving them to achieve their goals. You see, money will only drive a person on a superficial level, but personal fulfilment is long-lasting. This is why there are a very select few coaches who can actually deliver that experience to their clients.

When you genuinely invest the time in understanding what's happening with someone on a deeper level, you will always achieve an outcome that is built on trust. A few years ago, one of my clients in Sydney referred me to a friend of theirs in Melbourne who was experiencing some challenges with their business partners and were in desperate need of help. The work culture had become quite toxic and the business was suffering. I arranged a meeting, flew to Melbourne and sat in a café with them for seven hours, but not once did we discuss my services or fees. The entire time was spent understanding what the core issues were and how we could address them moving forward.

I focused on ensuring that they understood how this relationship had become toxic and what was required to turn it around, not on my fees or terms of engagement. I worked with this client for three-and-a-half years where we built a great relationship and achieved some great outcomes, all on the back of my initial investment of time, getting to understand what was going on at a much deeper level. This same process of investing time in building rapport and getting to understand the client and their business has held true for me with over 90% of my clients, which is why I say it is a privilege to work with them. By putting in effort upfront, you create a solid foundation to build on later. Adopting a cookie-cutter approach is like building a house on sand; it's not going to stand up for very long.

Now, while the use of technology certainly helped, the value of the engagement came from the trust that was built in our initial stages, which gave them the confidence that I was the right person to guide them and their business. This is a strategy that I have applied consistently. There have been numerous occasions when a client was not ready at that point and needed to feel more pain before engaging me, which could sometimes be 12 months after our initial discussion, but that initial conversation would stick, and that's what counts the most.

Investing time upfront also allows me to gauge if I really want to work with a client. While having someone pay my monthly fee is great for the bank account, they may not necessarily be someone I want to work with. And regardless of how much money they're willing to pay me, I don't work with a client if our values aren't aligned, it's as simple as that.

The more time you invest in a relationship, be it personal or commercial, the better the outcome becomes. It's like putting money in the bank; the longer you leave it there the more interest you accumulate, and in the same way, the more you put into a relationship, the more you get back in return. Why most people tend to fail, though, is they're not willing to put in the necessary time upfront. When you plant a seed, you don't expect to pick the fruit the very next day; it takes time, the seed requires nurturing, water, fertilizer, love and attention and the more love and attention you give it, the stronger the plant becomes and what you eventually reap is bigger, better and healthier fruit.

The same applies to any relationship, whether it's with your parents, spouse, children, friends or clients. The more you put into building and nurturing, the stronger the relationship becomes. Mother Nature has a beautiful way of teaching us that no matter what happens on the outside, it's what's underneath that matters, what's at the core that allows the blossoming to occur.

A great example is a bushfire. We've all seen the devastation that fire can cause to a forest, yet in time, that forest regrows and becomes healthy again, precisely because of the strong support system it has underneath the surface which comes from the nurturing it received in the initial growing stages that allowed the tree to develop a strong foundation of roots. Life is the same. A strong solid foundation beneath you will empower you to overcome the challenges that are thrown at you, so you emerge bigger, better and stronger than ever before.

Your Life In Reflection

- The more time you invest in a relationship, be it personal or commercial, the better the outcome becomes. It's like putting money in the bank; the longer you leave it there the more interest you accumulate. What are your relationships like?

- The more a plant is nurtured, the stronger it grows, and the same applies to relationships. The more you put into building and nurturing, the stronger the relationship becomes. When was the last time you stopped and reflected on your relationships and what they really mean to you?

The universe has a wonderful way of stretching us, allowing us to grow, when you find yourself wanting to give up is when you need to push through the most and allow the breakthrough to occur.

RALPH ANANIA

Chapter 6:

Overcoming
The Storms Of Life

S torms of life often hit when everything seems to be going well. Then all of a sudden and out of nowhere, your world can be completely turned upside down.

Many of us at some point will experience tragedy in our lives. Whether it be the loss of a loved one, a tragic accident, or the breakup of a long relationship, eventually and as hard as it is to do, we have to deal with the circumstances, take the time to grieve and deal with the loss, then put it behind us so we can move forward in life. This, however, is easier said than done, as there are multiple stages that you need to go through to get to a point where you can actually let go of whatever you're holding on to and be able to move forward.

On December 11, 2013, I was in Auckland, New Zealand, and had just wrapped up delivering a four-day business training event, when I received a call from my brother, Frank, with news that our mother had just passed away. I was very close to Mum, so the news rocked me to the core and all I wanted to do was get back to Sydney as quickly as possible so I could just go and see her one last time.

Unfortunately, between the time difference in New Zealand and the curfew at Sydney airport, it was too late to get on a flight and I had to wait until 6 a.m. the following morning. There I was in another country, alone in a hotel room, and all I could do was sit and wait all night. I had never cried so much in my entire life, and then I started the blame game, accusing myself of not spending more time with her, blaming myself for not being there to say goodbye, and a million other things.

The following 12 months were really tough, which I guess was to be expected when losing your mother, but with that also came the flow-on effects of all the 'firsts' that occur in the absence of a loved one. She had passed away just two weeks before Christmas, so it started with the first Christmas without her and just continued from there into 2014, which needless to say was a very tough emotional year. Unfortunately, everything has a breaking point and mine came nearly 12 months to the day, on a Sunday afternoon in December, when my wife of twenty-four-and-a-half years had come to a point where she no longer wanted to be in the marriage, and just like that, in an instant, the life I had come to know and love was gone forever.

This then triggered a multitude of emotions which saw me spiral into a very deep and dark place. I played the blame game again for a while, pointing an accusing finger at myself for working too hard, not being there enough, not supporting her emotionally, along with a million other things. Then when I was done on myself, I started blaming everyone else who may have played their part in it. Regardless of who played a part, the fact is that while there are always three sides to a story (yours, theirs and the truth), one has to take accountability for one's own actions, and this was certainly no different for me.

I was so desperate for answers that I started my journey in seeking help to get me through what was to be one of the toughest and most challenging seasons of my life. I have always relied heavily on my faith and belief in God, and let me tell you, I prayed more than I ever had, desperately longing to have my wife back and life to be as it was before. The next 12 months were a blur of appointments to see grief counsellors, medical psychiatrists, psychotherapists, hypnotherapists, spiritual healers, and I even had numerous discussions with the local priest. I read dozens of books and listened to a ton of podcasts on how best to navigate through this period, as I desperately wanted answers and wouldn't stop until I got them.

My challenge was that every time I sat across one of these people, I found myself analyzing them, which didn't help me of course and, in the end, the only thing that truly got me through was my faith. I had to come to a point where I needed to just let go and let God guide me through the journey. I did everything I possibly could and fought harder emotionally than I had ever fought for anything in my life, but unfortunately it just wasn't enough.

It's not where you expect to be at fifty years of age, having to start all over again so to speak, but it comes down to how you approach it and then get through it, especially when children are involved. It's quite amazing how resilient kids can be and the impact they can have when you're going through challenging times. The separation hit them pretty hard as we were (and still are) a very close-knit family, but you just got to keep pushing through. My relationship with my children became stronger and better, and step by step, day by day, we made the best of the situation and grew closer together creating new experiences and new memories along the way.

There I was at fifty having to learn to do all the things that I had taken for granted. There were some overwhelming times in the beginning—a few clothes that got destroyed in the wash, a couple of meals that were not quite perfect—but fast forward six years and we've well and truly found our rhythm, and all three of my children have grown to be such absolutely amazing young adults that I couldn't be prouder of them.

Life has a wonderful way of teaching us lessons that come in many different forms. A lot of times, you can reflect and beat yourself up for what you could've done differently, but that doesn't serve you. You need to accept that what has happened did so for a reason and that God has a bigger plan for you, that He needed you to learn this lesson before opening new doors for you. The more you fight it, the longer it takes for those new doors to open.

My duty as a father was to continue to show my children the unconditional love that I have for them and help them to be the best and strongest version of themselves. And as I said earlier, I couldn't be any prouder of all three of them. Michaela, my eldest daughter, is a very talented musician with an incredible voice and is making her mark as an amazing schoolteacher with her father's entrepreneurial flair. Alexandra, my middle daughter, has such a beautiful soul and is currently studying medicine. Christopher, at the time of writing this book, has just finished year 12 and has excelled in everything he's put his mind to; the world is his oyster, given that he is a talented footballer, and embodies natural entrepreneurial and leadership skills. All three are quite different, but also very astute in their own right.

Regardless of what was happening for me internally during the tough post-divorce years, the most important thing was to ensure that they felt loved and had stability. I put my life on hold to make sure that they navigated their way through this period as best as they could and with all the support they needed. There have been many adjustments along the way, and still many more to come as that's just part of growth. Time does heal all wounds but the scars remain forever. You need to keep pressing forward and not get caught up in chasing something that isn't there any-more; otherwise, you will never be ready to walk through the doors of new opportunity and possibilities when they present themselves and open up for you.

While a separation is never easy for either partner, it is extremely important that the kids don't get dragged into your dirty laundry. There will be anger, frustration and even resent-ment, which the kids will pick up on and you will want to share, but in the long run, it doesn't serve either side. As I mentioned earlier, there's always three sides to the story: yours, theirs and the truth. As long as the kids know that the separation was not their fault and that you love them unconditionally, that's all that matters.

Regardless of what happened to the marriage, children still need their mother as well as their father. You must never forget that, nor should you ever take either away from them, just because you want to hurt your partner; that is total stupidity. One thing that I am extremely grateful for is that my ex-wife and I never had any issues regarding the children as we both understood the importance of both parents being present in their lives.

Anyone who has been through a divorce may understand this from an emotional perspective; however, everyone's circumstances are different. The length of time you were together, whether you've had children together, the age of the children— all of these play a big part and make for individual circumstances and obstacles that will make every situation quite different. The unfortunate part of a divorce is when you have everyone else wanting to give their opinion, which then casts a shadow of confusion on what should and shouldn't be the right decision. If you get to that point, you are left with no choice but to involve lawyers, which just ends up burning through cash, leaving a very bitter aftertaste for everyone involved.

While there is still an element of sadness to everything that happened, I have no ill feelings towards my ex-wife. She gave me and helped raise three amazing children that I'm forever grateful for. I have come to understand and truly believe that God puts people in our lives for a reason and a season, and some of those seasons are longer than others. In our case, we had come to a point where we just grew apart and while all the signs might very well have been apparent, I was too focused on myself to see them and just took the relationship for granted in many ways.

Hindsight is a wonderful thing. Yes, if I had my time again, I would do things differently, but I don't, and therefore I need to learn from the experience and move forward. Yesterday is gone and can't be changed, but you do have the power to make tomorrow whatever you want it to be and that's where you must focus mindfully.

When I look back and reflect, I can clearly see why most people who have experienced a marriage breakup never move forward and tend to live life blaming everyone else. The first step in solving a problem is admitting that there is one, and then being open and willing to learn. You will never glean the lesson if you believe there's 'nothing wrong' with you and you're not open to learning.

Your Life In Reflection

- Life has a wonderful way of teaching us lessons and those lessons come in many different forms. A lot of times, you can reflect and beat yourself up for what you could've done differently, but that doesn't serve you. What lessons can you reflect on, look at from a positive perspective and use for good?

- Hindsight is a wonderful thing, but yesterday is gone and can't be changed. You *can* change tomorrow, and you have the power to make it whatever you want it to be; that's where you must focus mindfully. Where is your focus right now and how is it serving you?

Don't let what you experienced yesterday stop you from realizing the success that is waiting for you tomorrow.

RALPH ANANIA

Chapter 7:
Living Beyond Your Ego

The ego is quite complex; it can make us do awe-inspiring things and then on the flipside can also make us unhappy. Some of the most successful people I have ever met have massive egos, but they are also quite miserable, because regardless of how successful they are it's never enough and they always want more. So the cycle for them never ends, and sadly they rarely ever find peace.

One of my favorite teachers who I drew much inspiration from was Dr Wayne Dyer, and he would refer to ego as 'Edge God Out.' In a lot of ways, this is so true and the reason why so many successful people are empty. They can never find happiness because they have lived their entire life based around possessions. You see, the first part of EGO drives the belief that you must 'have more' to uphold your success.

The flow-on effect from that is if you are what you have, then when those possessions go away you lose yourself too. The other part of EGO drives the belief that you are what you do, so then your whole world revolves around what you do, which then leads to always wanting more 'things', because EGO has you believing that's what success is. This ends up becoming a vicious cycle where one needs to uphold an image or presence, which is built on material things.

Unfortunately, society has taught us that we need to 'compete.' Therefore, everything we do becomes about competition. Then what happens is that we start our journey through life based on what 'society' has told us about how we should be, how we need to look and how we should act. Over time, we get so caught up in the EGO that we lose all authenticity, we become so well-conditioned to be that way that it consumes us, making us believe that's who we really are. And it's only when you reach that point in your life, where you now have the 'look' and all the material 'things' except happiness, that you come to the realisation that you have no idea of what your real purpose in life is. And being a good businessperson that makes a lot of money is not a purpose.

Now don't get me wrong, there is a good side to the ego, as the ego can also protect you. The challenge though is finding balance. There was a time in my younger years when ego played a huge part in my life, but I have quickly come to realize that when you achieve something with the right intention, the ego falls away and humility shines through. The only time ego comes into play is when you need to prove to someone else that you've achieved more and therefore know more than they do, but in most cases, you end up looking like a fool and everyone around you sees it, except you. Sadly enough, I've seen many people in these situations, and nowadays I just call it for what it is and disconnect from that person, because life is far too valuable and way too short to get caught up in that materialistic and fake world.

The ego is also driven by what other people think or say about you, which in itself definitely won't serve you. My dad was highly respected in his community, so God forbid if we children ever did anything that would give someone the opportunity to gossip about him or our family. This was a real challenge.

When you start living a life worrying about what other people think, that belief is embedded into your subconscious as you grow older. You need to dress a certain way, act a certain way and live life a certain way—all because you worry about what people are going to say or think about you. Let me just say: the day I woke up to the fact that what people think of me is none of my business was the day the chains came off and I was free.

There will always be someone who will want to talk about you, and if you let that bother you, then everyone else around you will miss out on all the good you have to offer. Hand on heart, I couldn't care less what people say or think of me today, because there will always be someone who doesn't like how you look, how you speak or is jealous of you for something that you have absolutely no idea about.

Usually, these people have massive issues of their own and are just using any means they can to justify where they're at in life. To be honest, there are times when I look at someone and become quite sad, because I can see that deep down they are quite miserable and actually hurting. And as much as you would like to, you can't always help them, as their ego just won't allow it and they end up being hurtful towards you because they believe you are trying to have one over them.

We are all born with a unique DNA and, therefore, we are also put on this earth with a purpose. Sadly though, most people tend to just stroll through life living someone else's purpose and always feeling compelled to prove their worth, which only continues to feed their ego.

While I have entrepreneurial blood running through my veins and have built many successful businesses over the years, I found my true gift and purpose in helping others transform their lives. Regardless of the circumstances, whether in business or personal, life is life. God has put me on this journey to help those who need encouragement and guidance in finding their purpose, so they too can live a fulfilled life. I have been blessed with the opportunity to share my wisdom and experience, helping thousands of people around the globe find their purpose. I could never have achieved that if I had let my ego, or what people think, control me.

While I don't have a formal degree, I have spent years and invested hundreds of thousands of dollars in continually learning to better understand how to deliver my message to those who are desperately seeking help. And there is no better teaching resource than real-life personal experience, going through the journey yourself to better understand what and where you can improve. Sharing my experience with someone empowers them to go away and really blossom and become a much better version of themselves.

There's a saying that "good things come to those who wait." This is such a load of rubbish and reminds me of the story I once heard, which goes like this:

A storm descends on a small town, and the downpour soon turns into a flood. As the waters rise, the local preacher kneels in prayer on the flooded church porch. By and by, one of the townsfolk comes up the street in a canoe.

"Better get in, Preacher. The waters are rising fast."

"No," says the preacher. "I have faith in the Lord. God will save me."

Still, the waters rise. Now the preacher is up on the balcony, wringing his hands in supplication, when another guy zips up in a motorboat.

"Come on, Preacher. We need to get you out of here. The dam wall is gonna break any minute."

Once again, the preacher is unmoved. "I shall remain. The Lord will see me through."

After a while, the dam wall breaks and the flood rushes over the church until only the steeple remains above water. The preacher is up there, clinging to the cross, when a helicopter descends out of the clouds, and a state trooper calls down to him through a megaphone.

"Grab the ladder, Preacher. This is your last chance."

Once again, the preacher insists the Lord will save him.

And, predictably, the preacher drowns.

A pious man, the preacher goes to heaven. After a while he gets an interview with God, and he asks the Almighty, "Lord, I had unwavering faith in you. Why didn't you deliver me from that flood?"

God shakes his head and says, "What did you want from me? I sent you three life-lines—two boats and a helicopter. What more did you want me to do?"

Good things don't come to those who 'wait'; good things come to those who 'create' them with the right intention. When you create success—however that looks like for you, be it through personal wealth or fame—with the right intention, life becomes much more fulfilling and purposeful. There are a lot of wealthy and famous people in our world who are humble and extremely happy in life, but we don't often hear about them because their stories don't make the 'news.'

Regardless of what your purpose is, be it professionally or personally, when you do what you do from the heart, authenticity shines through. You will achieve a lot more in life being real and authentic than you ever will coming from a place where ego controls you.

If you find yourself going through the self-torture of allowing your ego to control you, then the following affirmations will help you.

1. You are not your thoughts and not your emotions

   You are the consciousness that witnesses your thoughts and emotions. Get this, and you get the fact that you and the things that happen around you are separate. This is good news, because you recognize that you are not your ego.

2. It's not personal

   Avoid taking things personally. The most powerful tool to let go of your ego is learning to not take it personally and practicing forgiveness.

3. Practice gratitude

   Being grateful for what you have will free you from focusing on what you believe you should have. Take a few minutes each day and think about all the people, experiences, lessons and mistakes you are grateful for.

4. Let go of your need for control

   We are not our egos, we are not our jobs, we are not our material possessions, and we are not our achievements. Once you let your ego control your life, you will never be happy or relaxed because as soon as you lose one of the things that you identify with, the rest will fall like dominos and you will lose your happiness. Break the fears fencing you in and trust life! Don't be scared to love. Take risks. Be curious. Explore. Do what makes you happy. Try to do something every day that stretches your boundaries, and you'll start to feel happiness in the little things.

5. Enjoy time alone with yourself

   Create a daily routine to remind yourself why it's so wonderful to be you. Take 15 minutes out of your day to be with yourself in silence, because sometimes it is only in silence that you can find the answers that you never could hear amidst the noise.

The most important thing to remember is that the ego creates negativity and thrives on the drama it creates out of nothing. That's not what you want in your life, because whatever you focus on and give attention to will grow. Water doesn't know the difference between a flower and a weed, it will feed both equally; the same applies to your energy. It doesn't know the difference between what's positive and what's negative, so be mindful of where you focus your attention, because what you feed will grow.

Your Life In Reflection

- Regardless of what your purpose is, be it professionally or personally, when you do what you do from the heart, authenticity shines through. You will achieve a lot more in life being real and authentic than you ever will coming from a place where ego controls you. Take some time now and define what your real purpose in life is. How will you use it for good?

The success of an organization starts with building a great team. It's not just about everyone on that team being happy, it's about being meaningful. Everyone wants to belong and once they have a sense of belonging, they become happy, and business thrives.

RALPH ANANIA

Chapter 8:

Surround Yourself With The Right People

G rowing a business can be quite challenging at the best of times, but the formula for running a successful business is the same, no matter what industry you're in; the only thing that changes is the product. The secret is that it requires great business skills, and the biggest reason that most start-ups collapse within the first couple of years is the lack of 'business' skills. Unfortunately, most entrepreneurs are focused on making it to the top as quickly as possible. And just like we see on the road signs while we're driving, 'speed kills' applies in business as well.

To grow a business, regardless of its industry or size, the first and foremost requirement is passion. If you're not passionate about what you're doing, then why are you doing it? The next necessity is a plan. You must have a plan that clearly articulates what is required to get you where you want to go and what you want to achieve. And then of course there needs to be purpose, a vision, and most importantly, you must do your research, as this will allow you to understand what is actually happening in your particular industry.

Most people who start a business have a delusion that just because they have great skills in their craft or profession— whether they are a great chef, a mechanic, a great builder, a plumber, or even a great doctor—they automatically have the skills to run a business. Being a great doctor doesn't make you a great businessman or businesswoman. It requires great business skills to run a successful business, just as it requires great medical skills to become a great doctor.

During my 30-plus years in business, I have seen numerous businesses fall by the wayside through lack of business experience and the need to act quickly. This really saddens me, because I believe that it's the small business sector that keeps a country's economy moving forward, and the reason that quite a lot of them go bankrupt is that no one was there to show them how NOT to go bankrupt.

I have seen many young entrepreneurs with a belly full of passion go and start a business only to fall flat on their faces, because they had no idea how to run a business or were too focused on having the title. Then we have the other side of the equation, where some people are happy to buy an established business and spend the money on purchasing it, but then don't 'want' to spend the money to learn how to run the business. If it's a franchise, the franchisor trains them on how to run the processes, be it baking bread or making coffee, and while it has changed somewhat in recent years, it is still very rare that they train them on how to actually run a successful business.

It was for this very reason that I created my *Boost Your Business* program many years ago, which I successfully delivered to audiences in 14 different countries during that time, to give SMEs an opportunity to come together with like-minded people and learn from someone who has been in their shoes and done it for over 30 years and knows what could go wrong and what will go wrong if you don't plan and apply the systems and processes that will keep your business on track.

Then we have the business owners who become complacent just because their business has been doing quite well financially for a number of years, just ticking along and making a profit. They've become comfortable and haven't kept up with modern trends or technology, so they eventually find that their business is starting to unspool and go backwards. They then blame everything on the economy or whatever is making the headlines at the time, rather than staying relevant and innovative and ahead of the competition.

Running a successful business does not have to be that difficult. It's just like being a world-class athlete who is at the top of their game. Firstly, they all have a coach and, secondly, they need to keep training to remain competitive. They rarely ever become comfortable and the same applies in business. When you reach that point where you've become comfortable in your business, you've actually become complacent and are starting to go backwards without even realizing it.

To become successful in business, you need a good coach and/or mentor. A good coach will always have you playing outside your comfort zone, not to the extent of making it unbearable, but you do need to be uncomfortable. What this means is that you are always looking at correcting, refining and making small adjustments to keep you focused and on top of your game, to stay innovative and find new trends. What worked last year won't automatically work next year or the year after that.

Surround yourself with a great team and listen to their input. If they are trained correctly and fully understand what your goals and aspirations are for your business, they will become your biggest asset. Listen to your clients and keep asking if you are meeting their needs, what you can do better for them, what changes they would like to see in your business and why.

The challenge we have today is that everyone likes to label themselves as a 'CEO.' There are so many solopreneurs out there who give themselves the title of CEO that I find it very amusing. A solopreneur with a CEO title is nothing more than the Chief 'Everything' Officer, and you will struggle to build a business of any size or significance by doing everything yourself. Now honestly, there may be a time when you find yourself doing everything, and that's okay if you recognize that it's for a temporary period to propel your transition to the next stage, but you won't grow if you stay there.

Being a real CEO is not about the title at all; it's about having a vision of where the business or organization will grow towards, and the leadership skills to bring your entire team onboard and make them believe in the same vision, have them own it and being able to lead them to become leaders themselves. The role of a CEO can be the hardest or the easiest in an organization, it all depends on the team you have around you.

While it took me a long time to create one, I have had some phenomenal human beings on my team, which certainly allowed me to be the visionary I wanted and create a path for growing the businesses I had, but it was the strength of the team that actually made it happen. You must believe in your team though, because if you don't, then you're wasting your time and it will show in the overall culture.

I have worked with organizations that have created such a toxic culture that it's accepted as 'just the way it is.' Unfortunately, all that does is eventually cause the demise of the business. I have always adopted the view that when you put someone in a position, make sure they have the right tools and all the support they need to ensure they succeed. You can have the best product and the best price, but if your team doesn't believe in you or the business, this will flow right through to the customer or client, and it will only be a matter of time before the customer or client will go looking for an alternative. Building a great team is the most crucial part of building a great business.

It's no different to building a sports team. If you don't create a winning culture where everyone is on the same team playing for each other, you will never win the game. And when you have a CEO who becomes too obsessed with themselves and their position and forgets about their team, you will never build a successful business, because having a 'champion' player on the team will not win you games. Developing a champion team where every player is giving their best for each other will always win games.

Putting in the time and investing in the team with training and upskilling will bring long-term gains for the entire organization, which will then build a great culture and reverberate all the way through to the customer or clients. As a CEO and entrepreneur, I have been challenged many times over the years, as I believe that the most important people in your business are your team members and not the customers.

My reasoning is that when you train your team members correctly, so that they're on the journey with you where they really embrace the vision you have for the business, the customer or client becomes the most important person to them. It's no good having the customer as the most important person in the business when your staff couldn't care less about them. Focus on your people by giving them the appropriate training and required guidance and leadership, motivate them to want to be part of a winning team, and the results will surely follow. As I said earlier, you will never grow a successful business on your own.

The same principles apply in life. When you surround yourself with the right people who encourage and support you, you will always succeed. Having negative people around, who are very opinionated and always disagreeing with everything you do or say, will not serve you in any way. You should love them just the same and remove them from your life.

Unfortunately, and sadly enough, these people generally have more issues than they admit and are usually jealous of everyone, regardless of the circumstances, because they see the world as owing them a living, instead of taking the necessary steps and appropriate action to correct their own life. Don't get caught up in other people's baggage, because they will happily hand it over to you if you let them and this will only weigh you down.

Your Life In Reflection

- Building a great team is the most crucial part of building a great business. It's no different to building a sports team. If you don't create a winning culture where everyone is on the same team playing for each other, you will never win the game.

- You will never grow a successful business on your own, and the same principles apply in life. When you surround yourself with the right people who encourage and support you, you will always succeed. Who are the people that surround you? Are they serving a purpose or merely taking up oxygen?

*Too often we try to accomplish something big,
without realizing that the greatest part of life is
made up of the little things.*

RALPH ANANIA

Chapter 9:

Handling Disappointments

'm sure you can relate when I say that in life, not everything will go according to plan. Be it in business, within the family or in relationships, you will encounter some level of disappointment. This can start at a young age, maybe with your parents, maybe if your teachers were bullies at school or your friends turned on you for no reason. This can also continue later in life; for example, someone you care about may turn against you, or you could be laid off a job that you love and are let go despite many loyal years of service. As Alexander Pope famously said, "Blessed is he who expects nothing for he shall never be disappointed."

When you get disappointed it can hurt. Sometimes a little, sometimes a lot. It can also drag you down, leaving you feeling quite flat for days on end. Navigating through disappointment is pretty tough to do in a world that expects a lot from you. That said, if you learn how to deal with disappointment in a healthier and more helpful way, then it can be a lot less painful and actually act as a springboard to learning from the experience, allowing you to grow.

If you're someone who's wired to expect the best, and then are let down and don't get it, the resulting disappointment and let-down can actually trigger a physiological response in the brain, especially if you have a tendency towards depression anyway. If you're finding it harder to get up and brush yourself off and start over, it might be because your brain is physically prevent-ing you from doing so. Remember though, just because you've had a setback or made a mistake, you are not a disappointment or a failure. And the situation you find yourself in will not last forever, even though it may feel that way right now or at the time.

Choosing to stay put in disappointment is never a good idea. Think about the event that's happened. It's in the past, so you can't influence it or change it. You can certainly ruminate over it and replay the many, many things you should've, could've and would've done differently if circumstances were different. However, the reality is that if you are reading this, it's likely that the disappointment is in your rear-view mirror.

There are things you can do to relieve yourself of disappoint-ment from a past event and prepare yourself for any disappoint-ments that are likely to come in the future.

So let's take a look at how you can move out of disappoint-ment and into more peace and happiness. You can accept that disappointment happens to everyone—it happened to you, no big deal. It can be helpful to start by normalizing the situation. No one gets through this life without some form of disappoint-ment; some are bigger than others, but everyone experiences it one way or another. Know that you are in good company and accept your state as perfectly normal.

Instead of brooding in your state indefinitely, once you have allowed yourself to acknowledge that you are in good company, start the process of reframing. Reframing means taking any situation and putting a more objective 'frame' around it. It can be helpful at this step to actually write your disappointment down, like journal notes. Record what happened but capture it like a journalist. Be clinical. Trying to separate the emotions from what happened is helpful to getting some personal power back.

Change your self-talk. Instead of telling yourself that this was the worst thing that could happen to you, shift your language to something more powerful (yet still true). "It happened, and now I need to figure out my next steps." Or "Disappointment happens to everyone, but it doesn't have to stop me from moving on." Or "I'm disappointed, but who dictates that I have to wallow in it? I can do something differently right now if I choose." Any time you hear yourself saying, "It's the end of the world" or "I can't go on" or "I'm a terrible person with bad luck", allow these phrases to act as the trigger to shift the talk to something more positive.

You can create a plan. Having a way to move forward when you've been thwarted and are feeling stuck is important. Don't make grand plans—"I'm going to move to the Bahamas and start a new life"—unless you have the will and the means to do so. Instead, start small; set a goal of something you can accomplish and move confidently in that direction. Experiencing some form of accomplishment, however minor, can send the message to your mind and your emotions that you can do it, so go ahead and do it. Remember, 'small' things consistently done will achieve extraordinary results. Don't try and change your world in one day, just do something small each day that will put you on the path to gaining extraordinary results.

Life is definitely going to test you, and possibly even throw more disappointments your way as you move away from the most recent one, but don't let that stop you from taking the lessons you've learnt from the experience and grow. Sometimes, to grow, we have to take risks, which means you need to step out of your comfort zone and stretch yourself. You will never achieve the growth and success you deserve if you live your life wrapped up in cotton wool. The lessons you learn from disappointment will make you look at life differently. There will always be those who don't hold the same values as you, and therefore disappointment is inevitable. Just don't allow that disappointment to control the outcome you want.

My focus has always been to ensure I can prepare my children as best as I can for what lies ahead, knowing that disappointment will at some stage rear its ugly head. I have had many conversations with my son Chris during our drive home after a disappointing football match, and my advice each time was to always remain humble and focus on the lessons learnt from this disappointment that will allow you to grow into a better person. Blaming the ref or the coach or the opposing team will not help, but when you look for the lessons and where you can improve, you will always come out on top. Looking at the same situation differently will always get you a better result.

If we take the time to teach this to our kids at a young age, it lays the foundation for how they approach and handle disappointment in the future, allowing them to assess the situation, deal with it straight away and then move on without any form of bitterness or regret. Guiding someone else through their disappointment also reinforces the message to our own selves, and that in itself is one of the greatest lessons one can obtain.

The last point I want to highlight here is regarding expectations. Your expectations can impact other people too. As far back as the 1960s, Harvard research demonstrated the power of our beliefs in swaying other people's behavior. When teachers in the study were told that certain (randomly selected) children were smart, those kids performed better not only in the classroom but also on standardized IQ tests, simply because the teachers expected them to do so. Your expectations, more than anything else in life, determine your reality. When it comes to achieving your goals, if you don't believe you'll succeed, then you won't, which will always raise disappointment.

Now can be a great time to assess where you may have some unrealistic expectations of yourself and of others in your life. You may need to reassess and determine what is realistic and what changes you need to make to avoid any potential disappointment. Write a list of what has disappointed you in the past when expectations were not met and why, as this will allow you to be more conscious of your expectations moving forward. What we're looking for here are patterns that may have developed over time without you realizing it, that you can now be aware of and change if and when required.

Expectations affect our emotions, and when they're not met can create dis-ease. Quite often, this happens without you even realizing, which then flows into your actions. Once you become aware of this and make the necessary changes to avoid any possible disappointment, your energy flows much better, your productivity increases, and you become more content and happier within yourself. Most of us tend to lose sight of our own awareness as it can often come with an element of pain. This is usually related to the fear of unfulfillment, and therefore we repeatedly and unconsciously keep pushing it aside. Self-awareness can be uncomfortable at times; however, it will stretch you and allow you to grow in areas that you may not have realized before.

I just want to close off with this: Self-awareness is simply the capacity to observe ourselves. What you can do from now on is pay more attention to the patterns within your thoughts, feelings and behaviors. This will allow you to have better relationships, make better decisions, become more effective in your communications and increase your overall productivity—which all lead towards eliminating disappointments.

Your Life In Reflection

- No one gets through this life without some form of disappointment; some are bigger than others, but everyone experiences it one way or another. Know that you are in good company and accept your state as perfectly normal. Where has this shown up for you in your life and what can you do to change it?

A person can always make money, but Money doesn't make a person.

RALPH ANANIA

Chapter 10:
The Value Of Money

"**M**oney is the root of all evil." I'm sure you've heard someone you know say this. Well, let's just bury that right now, because it's not true. People who say this usually don't have any money and that's just their way of justifying it. Money is the by-product of how well you have applied yourself to creating the life you want; how you then use it is what determines its true value.

If you choose to invest it to grow your wealth so you can do great things and help a good cause, then it's certainly not the root of all evil. Why some believe this false notion is because they have had a bad experience with money, which usually stems from the fact that they didn't know how to manage it and did something stupid that gave them an undesirable outcome. However, instead of looking internally to what drove them to making that wrong decision, they blame it on the money, which is totally wrong.

There are a few fundamentals that are important to note around money though. Money doesn't make you a smarter or better person or more superior than someone else. Money may allow you to have more material things, but it doesn't make you a better person. The world is full of people who hide behind their wealth and look down on anyone who is not at their financial level. That's not generalizing it, for I also know many wealthy individuals who are extremely humble with a massive heart and live a very balanced life.

They have worked extremely hard to get to where they are in life and may be able to afford more expensive things, but they have a real appreciation for money and will never flaunt it. Ultimately, it comes down to understanding what value you place on money and how you choose to live your life because of it.

When you can learn how to take care of your money, your money will take care of you. What I mean by that is, keep a personal budget so you can always track your money, then identify what and where is the best place for you to invest in. Always start small, test and measure, understand what you're investing in and then make better decisions about whether you want to invest more or take your investment out. If you're looking to invest in a business, make sure you do your due diligence and don't leave any stone unturned.

There will always be bright shiny objects that will distract you, but you need to look beyond them and go deeper into why you are willing to invest in this business and assess if it will give you the financial return you're looking for. There have been many cases where people invest in a business but haven't done their due diligence, only to find that all they did was 'buy' themselves a job and become a 'slave' to their investment.

Sadly enough, and in most cases, that scenario usually doesn't end well. I have seen many a couple who have invested their entire life savings into a business they knew nothing about, didn't do any due diligence, worked seven days a week to try and make a go of something, only to lose it all a year or two later. What's even worse is the flow-on effect, because it then also affects their marriage and in extreme cases even destroys their family.

I loved woodwork as a subject at school and always remember my woodwork teacher who would say, "Measure twice and cut once." This applies to everything in life. Always measure twice before cutting, meaning that whenever you are making a decision that will impact many areas of your life, make sure you 'measure' and look at everything in great detail, then go back and look at it again to see if you've missed anything. Because once you've 'cut' and handed your money across, any issues or misleading that crop up will cost you, forcing you to spend a lot of money and your very valuable time in court trying to get your investment back.

I have worked with a number of clients who were sold a business that looked good on paper—their accountant didn't do the appropriate due diligence as they will usually only assess what's put in front of them and then sign a disclaimer taking zero responsibility—and ended up taking the previous owner to court. The outcome is rarely a good one, because the previous owner will also have their own disclaimer stipulating that the buyer needs to perform their own due diligence.

This means that missing out on one technicality can leave the purchaser with a business that they've overpaid for. What tends to happen then is that the legal fees keep accumulating and getting out of control, so the purchasers are totally deflated and get to a point where they don't even want anything to do with the business anymore and are prepared to just cut their losses and walk away.

Now this may seem like doom and gloom, but it doesn't mean you should never buy or go into a business, not at all. A business will give you a greater return than most other forms of investment; the risk is higher and therefore the return is also much higher. When you have the right support around you, business can be a lot of fun. I would highly recommend a good coach or mentor who has been there and knows what to do, who can guide you and hold your hand along the way. It will keep you motivated and make you inspirational to others, because if you're happy and love what you do, so will those around you. You can also become quite creative and look for ways to keep ahead of your competitors with innovative ideas, which again is quite exciting and keeps you enjoying what you do. When you enjoy what you do, it's not a job anymore. It becomes a way of life.

Money doesn't fix problems. Sure, there are times when money will make a problem go away, but it doesn't fix it. Fixing a problem requires communication, compromise, solution and negotiation. Money won't fix a broken relationship; what's required there is better communication and a willingness to compromise. Money won't make you happy; what you do with it might make you happy for a little while, but once again, the world is full of very wealthy individuals who are unhappy and quite miserable.

How many times do we read in the media about someone who seemingly has everything but has taken their own life? Why? Because they may have had the financial wealth, but they never found happiness. Money can't reverse the death of a loved one or undo the outcome of a natural disaster. Money is merely a tool that will allow you to have certain things—and a great tool when used wisely.

Then there are those who are uncomfortable about making or having too much money. This is just a belief that will not serve you. As I said earlier, money is a by-product of how well you do certain things, and the better you are at it, the more money you will make. You would never chop down a healthy fruit tree because it's producing good fruit, so why would you stop doing what you do because you're making too much money? It's crazy, right?

I have often been challenged about my fees in the past—about why I charge at the price I do. My answer is that most people will focus on the value of what they're getting. If I can return my fee to the client by providing ten times the value they paid, my fee becomes irrelevant, because they received ten times more value than what they paid me. The challenge with society in general is that most people are always looking for that fast buck, so instead of looking at what value they can give, they look at what they can 'gain.'

Unfortunately, there are many so-called experts in many different industries who will promise their clients the world and deliver them an atlas. When this happens, we often use the term 'burn and churn.' They keep burning clients because they have a good marketing funnel that keeps bringing in new ones, so they don't care either way.

I've always maintained my integrity and will never promise what I can't deliver. There are many areas that I'm exceptional in, and then there are some that I'm not, but I make that very clear upfront so there is no expectation to deliver something I know I can't. Having spent over three decades in business, I have been able to surround myself with some exceptional professionals who are experts in their field, and I can therefore refer them to my clients knowing that they maintain my same level of integrity and will deliver the required outcome. That in itself is worth its weight in gold, because they have someone that they trust, making the entire process seamless and delivering real value to the client.

If you're considering going into business but have some reservations, I would definitely encourage you to get in touch. We can have a chat and see if we can get you some clarity on it. As I mentioned earlier, small businesses form the financial backbone to every economy, which keeps countries alive. When done properly, a small business can produce great results and give you the financial freedom you deserve while also letting you have a lot of fun at the same time.

Your Life In Reflection

- When you can learn how to take care of your money, your money will take care of you. How does that resonate with you? Take some time to reflect and reassess where you are right now financially and what changes you may need to make.
- Money doesn't fix problems. Sure, there are times when money will make a problem go away, but it doesn't fix it. That requires communication, compromise, solution and negotiation. Where has this played out in your life and what can you do to rectify it?

How you spend your mornings. How you talk to yourself. What you read. What you watch. Who you share your energy with. Who has access to you. These are the choices that will change your life.

RALPH ANANIA

Chapter 11:

Adapting to Change

We live in a very fast-paced world today where change is happening at lightning speed. Adapting to change keeps us relevant, valuable and at the forefront with a competitive edge. That said, adapting to change doesn't mean you need to change who you are at your core; it means you must make the adjustments required to grow with forward momentum.

I have always been able to adapt to change reasonably well, but there are those who find it quite overwhelming and go into complete shutdown. Regardless of whether we like it or not, change is inevitable. It's better to sit with it and understand what that change is going to look like for you, rather than putting your head in the sand and ignoring it altogether.

Changes occur in our lives for many reasons. Some appear through unforeseen circumstances, such as a sudden health challenge that may require you to make some unexpected changes to your lifestyle, and yet others are out of our direct control, such as a change of government introducing new policies that change what we've become accustomed to.

You could be made redundant at work, which will bring change to your financial circumstances, or you may get a promotion or a better job offer, which may require you to uproot your family and move to another state or country, bringing change into many areas of your life. Regardless of the circumstances and whether you are consciously aware of it or not, change is happening around us all the time.

That said, there are many things you can do to make a change easier to accept. First of all, it will certainly help if you look for the positives in every changing situation. This eliminates the stress that can sometimes be associated with change, be it an argument that you could have avoided or an outburst that you're going to later regret. It will also help you to avoid sleepless nights or elevating anxiety, which will over time negatively affect your health and well-being. All change comes with some form of emotional side-effect; the challenge is knowing how to address that emotion. When you can just sit back and take the time to assess the change and eliminate all the negative thoughts associated with it, you will be able to move forward and embrace the new change with open arms.

Whether I'm presenting on stage or working with clients, I encourage people to embrace change rather than fight it. Change is going to happen anyway, so even if you fight it, you'll just waste time and end up taking longer to achieve whatever it is that you're looking to achieve. Change is a good thing. Change is evolvement. You should understand that change is growth, regardless of how that looks for you today. When you really embrace change, things will flow more smoothly for you.

That said, there can also be times when change happens too fast and you're not prepared, something I've experienced a number of times in business, and this can have an adverse effect. Let me expand on that. If you've always been challenged by a lack of money, whether it's just getting by or having some tight situations to deal with, and all of a sudden in a short space of time, be it through a huge increase in business or suddenly receiving an inheritance, you've got your hands on a lot of money, you'll tend to go through it very quickly, being unable to hold onto it. I have seen this happen many times over the years.

Even people who claim they don't like change will shift their beliefs in an instant when a positive change happens. This is the reason why we see a lot of lottery winners lose all their money within a few years. They don't know how to handle it, and by this, I mean they've never been taught how to plan or invest correctly, or how to find the right investment, or be wise with it, because they don't understand those areas. The money is only a by-product of what we work hard at. What's important here is understanding the changes that come into your life around money and being aware of them. While money can give you a better *lifestyle*, it should never change you as a person.

Embracing change and adapting to financial change is simply utilizing your finances to move forward in life. In business and in life, people often focus on what they don't have rather than what they do have, and there are many ways people can go through life while adopting financial change. Some people are always in debt and they simply don't know how to adapt to change. It's not necessarily the finances, it's them adapting to the consequences of the way they handle any financial change that happens in their life.

It could be that they're struggling through tough economic times or it could be that they're overwhelmed with doing exceptionally well, but either way, such people can't adapt to change. This is because such people tend to live their life according to what they've become accustomed to. In business, and I've been through this myself. You may have a few really great years in which you've made a lot of money, so that you start to become accustomed to it and assume those times are going to continue forever. What happens is that it doesn't prepare you for when the challenging times come, and trust me, those challenging times *will* definitely come.

COVID-19 is a perfect example; as I sit here writing today, the entire planet is going through the most challenging time of the modern world. Unfortunately, as individuals, we were not prepared for this pandemic, but even under normal circumstances, assuming that those good times will never end will always lead to complacency. In business, when you become complacent, you start to make decisions based on today rather than the future, and this is why a lot of people that make money fast also lose it equally fast.

Back in the '90s, a lot of people became extremely rich quickly in the dot-com era. They thought it was so great that they kept investing on and on in dot-com shares, until they found out they were investing in nothing; the market collapsed, and they lost everything. The smarter ones who pulled out did make a lot of money. However, greed is another aspect of financial change. When is enough, enough? A lot of people get caught up in greed and no matter how much they have, it's never enough. You know, a $20,000 car does the same job as a $200,000 car. It may not have all the luxuries, but it will still get you safely from point A to point B just the same.

There are a lot of people in the world who have only ever had a $200,000 car, so when their financial situation changes and all of a sudden, they can only afford to drive a $20,000 car, they go into meltdown and think the world has come to an end because they've been deprived of something *material* and meaningless in life. Talk about material things with someone who has a very sick child and is in need of thousands of dollars each month for medical expenses and they will give you a very different perspective. This highlights the importance of being aware of the continual lessons you learn along the way, and how to take these lessons on board and adapt to change, regardless of how that looks for you.

When you look back over the years, you will find that a lot of businesses that do extremely well from the moment they start trading often vanish overnight, gone in a short space of time. Initially, it could be that they were in the right place at the right time, or they nailed it with the right product, or hit a great trend. What happens such businesses crash is that they have hit the ground running at lightning speed but failed to slow down enough to build a *sustainable* foundation. Building a business is exactly the same as building a house.

You need to have a solid plan, and when you have proper planning you will have identified the potential risks. Identifying risks does not always mean looking at the negative things, it's also about highlighting what will happen when you grow too quickly. Taking these risks into account allows you to develop a plan to mitigate those risks, which again will bring change.

One of the biggest challenges most people face is that they put all their focus on avoiding change. When I'm presenting and sharing my wisdom around building a business, I always ask the audience to raise their hand if they like change, and the number of hands that go up are always less than half the people in the room. I then explain that when you are faced with a problem, be it in business or even in your personal life, you need to find a solution to address that problem, issue, or challenge.

What happens when you find a solution? You automatically create *change*. So here's the lesson: every single time you find a solution, you will always automatically create change, so don't fight the change and always look for bigger solutions, because that's where growth comes from.

Your Life In Reflection

- Adapting to change doesn't mean you need to change who you are at your core; it means making the adjustments required to grow with forward momentum.
- Change is growth, regardless of how that looks for you today, and when you really take it on and embrace change, things will flow more smoothly for you. What can you change that will help you move forward in life?

*The decisions you make today
will not just affect your tomorrow
but will determine your future.*

RALPH ANANIA

Chapter 12:

Invest In Your Personal Growth

As a young child in school, you are taught that it's not good to make mistakes, and you soon learn that if you make a mistake, you're going to get into trouble. But then you go on through life believing that you can't make mistakes, or you shouldn't make mistakes. This can stop you from making a crucial decision, keep you from taking an element of risk later in life, or prevent you from trying harder than you normally would, because you're scared of making a mistake.

It's okay to make mistakes and necessary to learn from those mistakes, because that's what growth is. When we're fed the belief that it's *not* okay to make mistakes from a very young age, it changes everything about life. Unfortunately, we tend to live our lives fearing we *might* make a mistake, which holds us back from actually pushing through and trying harder. There's only a very small group of people who are naturally determined to push through barriers; the rest live in fear of taking the next step.

However, living in your comfort zone doesn't allow for personal growth. Personal growth comes from continually moving forward. It's okay to fail, but make sure to fail forward. Failure is not just about falling down; we fall down, we get up, and we get going again. Real failure is when people truly give up and there's no more moving forward—that's absolute failure.

Making mistakes or failing at something doesn't determine who you are as a person. Who you are is characterized by the way you deal with setbacks, and the way you get through tough times and challenges in your life. You need to understand that growing means transitioning through different stages of your life, and the very first stage where it all starts is your early years at school. Some of the things we're taught as children are not necessarily true; for example, 'practice makes perfect.' This is the biggest load of rubbish that anyone could take on board because only *perfect* practice makes perfect.

Now I wasn't a naturally gifted student at school and I'm sure many of you were the same. So, if a teacher would ask you to go home and practice a certain subject, a subject you're not necessarily good at and don't know how to get through, how does that make it perfect? You're effectively going to be practicing something you have no idea about, so you're going to be making all the same mistakes. This means practice doesn't make perfect, it just makes you more confused. You can only practice what you know is going to propel you forward, and you need to understand what is leading you in the right direction. Only perfect practice makes perfect, and that's the challenge we have as we transition through the different stages of our lives, because the beliefs instilled in us as children stay with us and resurface as we navigate through life as an adult.

To understand the different stages of life and how you're going to transition through them, it is important to have the right grounding and foundations. Growing up in an immigrant family, with parents who had come from another country with not a lot to start a new life with, was a challenge in itself, but it also meant that I had to navigate through the process of going to school pretty much on my own as they weren't necessarily checking my homework or keeping tabs on how I was doing. I just had to keep pushing through and do the best I could. However, when I look at my own children today, I can see that they've had a fairly solid foundation where their mother put in a lot of work in the early years, allowing them to grow and evolve, which is extremely important for children.

Christopher, my youngest child has just finished Year 12, his final year in school, where he's been in the same school since kindergarten. He's gone through the entire schooling process and progressed into leadership roles in school and in sport because he's had the ability to transition into each stage as the school years went by. He's been able to achieve what he has achieved because he's been able to continually learn, grow, make some mistakes, then learn from those mistakes and keep growing.

Being able to understand each component of your life and growing into it makes a huge difference. In school, you have an understanding of what you're working towards from one year to the next, so you're always looking forward and planning forward, and you understand what needs to be done to get to where you want to be and to achieve what you want to achieve. Life, however, does not work is such neat patterns and we often get too busy to notice where we're heading.

You need to know what's coming up and plan how you'll grow into it. Consider a couple who has a baby on the way. They know the baby is coming, so there is an element of preparation before the child arrives when they actually grow into that next stage of life, which is parenthood. This happens with obvious, big events in life, but it doesn't happen enough in everyday living. If we were to look at it in this way and plan forward, we could grow into every aspect of life from a personal perspective, meaning we won't end up getting to the age of 65 or 70, looking back thinking, "Wow, what have I really achieved? All I've been doing is working in a job for the last 40 or 50 years." Life is not about that; it's about you growing personally. It's okay to work in a job, but what are you doing *personally* that allows you to grow?

I've taken a lot of risks in my life, but I've always looked forward and looked to grow as a person because unless I'm growing, I can't help anybody else. To be able to help other people, especially my children, I've had to accept and embrace change and continue to learn more along the way. Today, I'm a coach and mentor in both the business world and in life in general because I've done the work myself and been through my own journey of personal growth. It's this that allows me to do what I do from a standpoint of real-life experiences, and not necessarily from the pages of a textbook.

A lot of people read and take lessons from textbooks, but it's fair to say that not every author of those textbooks will have gone through the experiences they write about. I'm not saying that the lessons learnt from textbooks are wrong; I'm saying that I've lived through challenges most people haven't gone through, and may never go through, and because of this I'm able to help people through real-life experience rather than textbook learning.

It's important to understand the personal growth you're gaining out of life, because your experience will help those around you, even if you don't realize that you're doing it. Personal growth is super important to continually move forward. Staying still will only lead to complacency. One of the biggest shifts that happened in my own life was when I started engaging mentors. I've had many wonderful mentors during my 30-plus years in business and the difference they make is huge. There are times in life when ego comes into the decisions you make, creating the need to look good around your peers and friends.

Having a mentor allows you to learn that this isn't the way to go about it. They see things you can't see because your ego is getting in the way, and they pull you up on those things, helping to bring balance into your life and encouraging you to grow. You can only ever gain balance in your life if you have someone there who looks at what you're doing and how you're doing it, and helps to point out what you need to do more of in one area and less of in another. This is what brings balance in your life. If you're working 20 hours a day and you're putting no focus on your family or on yourself in terms of well-being, then you don't have balance in your life.

If you are working hard, as well as spending time with your family *and* looking after your health and well-being—eating well, exercising, meditating or anything else—you'll find that you can achieve a lot more in lesser time because your focus is a lot clearer, your mind less cluttered, and you're bringing joy into your life. I have seen so many people in senior executive positions who are worth an absolute fortune, but they have not been there for their children throughout their younger years, and so, as they get older, those children don't want to know them. This is very sad. They've worked their entire life to give their children what they can, but they've missed the most important part, and that's spending time with them. It's the time you spend together that your children remember, not the money or material things.

My son Chris loves football. He's an exceptional player and in his final year at The King's School was appointed captain of the 1st Xl squad, a position that he worked extremely hard for. I did everything within my power to attend every game. I wouldn't miss a game, not only because it means a lot to me but also because it means a lot to him to see me there. I'm his biggest fan. What makes it more important is that the time I'm spending with him now will set the foundation for a stronger father-son relationship as we get older together. The time I've taken out to be involved in his life has allowed me to do more.

I was the president of the King's school football club, not because I wanted to be president (I was voted in) but because I wanted to be there to take a lead role in the club to support my son and his dream of playing football. Of course, there have been many times when making it to a game was a challenge, especially during the busy periods that happen in business, but you just have to make the time.

You balance it. You keep a diary, and you balance your time to be able to fit in what matters. It's important, more so for me because as my son finishes Year 12 this year and I won't have another opportunity to watch him play school football. It's at these pivotal times in life that a mentor can help you see what you can't see or what you might be overlooking, giving you the opportunity to navigate through each stage without making the mistakes you potentially would otherwise. Now, you're still going to make mistakes. If you want to take risks in life, you're going to have to accept that you will end up making some mistakes along the way, but when you navigate through those challenges and learn, you grow. That's *personal* growth. No one can take that away from you.

What most people fail to realize is that life skills are every bit as valuable as academic or professional skills. People go to college or university to pursue a degree or a profession and become the best they can be at it, and the things they learn stay with them forever. It's just the same with life skills, but most people don't value them in the same way.

Your life skills, that is, being a great parent, a great negotiator, a creative problem-solver, or a great listener, are your personal skills and have all contributed to your personal growth, but most people go through life without really valuing them. They value the position they hold or the product they've sold or the business they've grown, but they don't value the parts of their personality that allowed them to take their business or their profession to that level, when in fact that's personal growth. It's *all* personal growth.

So, the next time you look at yourself and say, "I don't really know what I'm good at or the difference I can make," go beyond the superficial, go beyond the material. You may have no business experience and maybe you didn't go through school or Uni the way you wanted to, but you could be a phenomenal mother, and that fact makes a massive difference in the world. That is something that has shone through my children, because they have a phenomenal mother who prepared them so well for what the world has to offer. How many other mothers are out there struggling, mothers who don't have motherhood sorted yet, and how many of those mothers could you make a difference to?

That's what's important, and that's where your value is. It's not about the material things; it's not about the certificates you've achieved or didn't achieve. It's about the difference you can make in the world. Your contribution to the world is the summation of everything you have learnt from your real-life experiences and your own personal growth. That's where your real value is. It's extremely important to recognize and embrace this real value, because NO ONE can take that away from you.

If you want to achieve anything in life, you have to believe in yourself and be able to take that leap of faith, put your neck out, and just move forward. Not everything you do is going to work out the first time, but that's what growth is. The first time I got up on a stage to speak was when I had been invited to speak about the innovation in my business, but I was not a speaker then, so I had no idea what I was doing. I just thought it would be great. I was all excited and I stepped up onto the stage. Then, I literally froze. I'd worked out exactly what I was going to present and how I was going to present it, but my mouth went dry the second I saw all those eyes looking at me…I struggled, *really* struggled, through it. What was meant to be a one-hour presentation, I did in eight minutes. That's what I ended up with, just eight minutes on stage. I'd missed 90 percent of what I was going to talk about, my mind had gone cloudy, and I just froze.

Had I allowed the fear of that day to set in, I wouldn't have gone through to do what I do today. Fast forward to many years later and I've been on stage hundreds of times, spoken to tens of thousands of people, often in front of audiences of thousands. People sometimes say to me, "I don't know how you do it, you're great, you're a natural." The thing is, I may seem like a natural today, but I became a natural because I put a lot of work into continually doing it—continually speaking and continually failing forward.

It's amazing how many times you're up on stage and you make a mistake. You know in your head it's not what you wanted, but you don't make a big deal, you just push through, and then you can go back and assess that later. I might watch a video of a presentation after an event and pick out the places where I went wrong, but the important thing is to just keep going, keep pushing forward. This is what matters. It's not about me or what I've been able to do, it's about getting up and doing it.

That first time I got up on stage and I froze, I must have looked like an idiot, but I didn't stop, nor did I let that one awful experience stop me from moving forward. There was a part of me that had to push past all of it to be able to make a difference. I knew my purpose was to share my message, and that was the most important part for me. I had to just keep pushing through, and I did, and I kept getting better and better and better. Today, it's a very different story. I get up on stage, I speak quite freely, and I don't even need to have a presentation.

I can't tell you the number of times I've been on stage in front of hundreds or thousands of people and there's been a technical issue of some sort that brings the presentation to a halt. It can happen, but you don't make a big deal, you just keep pushing through. My wonderful speech coach Jennifer Leonie once said to me, "The day you know you've made it is when things go wrong and you just carry on, because you know what you're doing and you know your message, and you're so focused on the outcome and getting the message across that no distraction or challenge is going to stop you from doing exactly that." And that's where I am today.

In telling you all of this, I hope to encourage you to recognize your own personal worth and bring it to the surface. What is it you're great at? What personal growth have you gone through in your own life experiences that is of real value? Don't ever let anybody tell you that you're not good enough or that you'll never amount to anything; that's their issue to contend with, not yours to hang on to. Personal growth is something to embrace and continue throughout life, regardless of your age or circumstances, because your personal growth can also inspire growth in others around you.

Your Life In Reflection

- The life skills you have—whether you're a great parent, a great negotiator, a creative problem-solver, or a great listener—are your personal skills and they have all contributed to your personal growth, but most people go through life without valuing them. What can you take away from this to value who you really are?

- Personal growth is something to embrace and continue throughout life, regardless of your age or circumstances, because your personal growth can also inspire growth in others around you. What changes can you make to ensure you're always growing?

It takes years of hard work and perseverance to become an overnight success. Most people tend to overlook the length of time it takes and only see the result.

RALPH ANANIA

Chapter 13:

Build Strong Foundations

H ave you ever driven past a vacant block of land in your local area, and then one day you notice a fence has gone up around the perimeter and you think to yourself, it looks like they're getting ready to build something there?

You then drive past a few weeks later and notice quite a bit of activity, maybe some excavators and other earthmoving equipment working away. Then for months, as you continue to drive past this property, you notice everything lying dormant; nothing seems to be happening. Then one day, as your drive past the property, you have to look twice to believe that all of the framework has gone up, and you think, wow, that's gone up really quickly. And yes, while it may *appear* that way, all those times you drove past and it looked like nothing was happening, was when a lot of what you can't physically see was actually taking place.

The foundations were being laid, all the pipes were being put in, and the concrete slab was given the required time to set. The foundations had to be made deep enough and solid enough to support the building, only then could the building go up without collapsing. The same applies in life and in business. There are those who start a business and from day one exceed all expectations and almost always don't have the time to build that necessary solid foundation.

It's like the business has taken off before they've actually laid the concrete, so even though the business is doing well, they're still trying to lay the concrete. The business keeps growing and there isn't any time for the concrete to actually dry. So as the business continues to grow, it sinks deeper into the concrete, which is neither dry enough nor strong enough to sustain the business's enormous growth.

It takes a solid foundation to ensure sustainability, to avoid 'failing' in any area of your life. As you continually build, you sometimes have to take a step back and look at what else you need or what you may have missed. Only then can you make the adjustment required to ensure those foundations remain solid enough, so you can continue to build your empire with the certainty that it's not going to collapse.

Foundations are important in every area of your life, whether it's personal, emotional or physical, and whether it's related to your health and wellbeing, or business and finances. Foundations sustain your growth, and solid foundations prepare you for a bigger brighter future. When you've got a really good foundation in every area of your life, even when challenges arise (and that's just life) and you slip back, you don't fall into the deep hole that a lot of people sometimes do when they've been challenged by adversity. If you've built solid health and wellbeing foundations, then you tend to recover fairly quickly even when faced with a health crisis, because you've taken the right measures throughout your life to ensure that if something was to happen, it's not going to affect you that badly.

As I write, I'm 56 years of age. I still get up every morning at 5 a.m. and head to the gym to train four or five days a week. I don't do it because I want to be a model, I do it to keep my body physically active. As we get older, we begin to experience different aches and pains, and it is movement that can help us through this process. Muscle is what carries your bones through, so by building muscle you protect your bones, which in turn builds a healthy foundation.

I often joke about it, saying that every birthday after you turn 50 brings a new ache or pain, but I don't get caught up in the doom and gloom of aging. I might feel aches and pains, and there are mornings when I really don't feel like getting out of bed, especially when it's freezing cold outside and my bed is nice and warm, but I push through. By the time I leave the gym, I'm feeling good and ready to start my day.

Sustainability plays a huge part in foundation. I often have clients who want to lose weight or get fit, but they almost always struggle to achieve this result. I point out that if I asked them to stop doing all of the things that they enjoy doing, the changes from that wouldn't last long, and they wouldn't be able to sustain it. It has to be sustainable, so if you're someone who is used to having six slices of bread every day, you would initially cut it down to four, then cut it down to two, but you wouldn't cut it out completely because then you'd be depriving yourself of something you've enjoyed.

You don't wake up one day and weigh yourself and find that you've put on 20 kilograms from the day before. Just like that increase in weight has happened over a long period of time, losing it will also take time. You need to do it in a way that allows you to enjoy the process, making it sustainable. This is the reason why a lot of health fads don't last. A lot of overweight people go on a diet, lose the weight, then put it all back on again, and this rollercoaster of ups and downs is because they've cut everything out too heavily and their body is deprived of it. The foundation is not set, it's not sustainable, and they'll inevitably feel the urge to revert to old ways.

What will happen is they'll lose 20 kilograms and think, "Well, I've worked hard and deprived myself of all the things I loved, so it's okay to have a piece of chocolate now," and because they've deprived themselves for so long, they can't stop. One occasional piece turns into one frequent piece, which then turns into a whole block—and even that's not enough to satisfy the craving, so then they go out and get a full-sized family block. And just like that, they'll start putting on the weight back again. Now, it *is* okay to have some chocolate, and it's okay to have one cheat day a week, but you can't have one day a week of eating well and six cheat days; that will never work.

This is the challenge with making sure that there is sustainability in what you're doing. If you don't find sustainability, whatever you're hoping to achieve is going to collapse. If you're training hard to develop the body you want, and then you like what you see in the mirror one day and decide not to train anymore because you're looking good, that's not going to work. Getting to that point is when you need to maintain the achievement. You don't need to push your body as hard, but you do need to maintain it. You need that maintenance to sustain you at that desirable level, and you're then supported by strong foundations.

Strong foundations are also crucial in all our relationships, even in business. Whether it's relationships with business suppliers, business partners, your staff or clients, these relationships are very important to build and maintain because they form the foundation of everything you do to allow your business to flourish. It's no good just having a business that's doing well if every area of that business lacks substance.

A business does well when it has the right foundations, which are built by having the right people in place. People who will help you build the business you want and come along on that journey with you. Having the right people on your team is about building relationships. This then flows into the relationships you build with your clients, a relationship of trust where the focus is not on price but on value additions. Your clients feel good in the knowledge that when they come to you, they're going to get looked after and get a great experience. It won't matter what money they're spending with you, because they appreciate that what they're paying for is worth far more than the value of the money they paid.

One unfortunate thing I see often is that a lot of people in business tend to focus on trying to screw over their suppliers. They want to screw their suppliers for everything they can get, but if you do that without leaving enough in it for them to make a living, they're going to go broke, and what good is that to you? You won't have the product, or you'll need to look for other suppliers, so your relationship with suppliers must have a good solid foundation that is built on trust. If a time comes when you need a special deal or a favor, or you need something in particular, the relationship should be strong enough for the suppliers to be willing and able to help you without any hesitation at all.

This is extremely important right across the board in business, and it also applies to relationships in life in general. Whether it's your friends, your spouse or partner, or your children, a lot of work goes into building those relationships. The more time and effort you put into building all areas of those relationships, the better and more fruitful a life you'll have. If there's an area in your life that's lacking, you need to go back far enough to see where the building of the relationship failed. If you build as you grow with that person, be it a friend, spouse, partner or your children, and you continually build on that relationship as a two-way partnership, you'll find that it will flourish.

When you invest the time in building a great relationship upon a solid foundation, you can speak openly to that person, so even if something undesirable were to happen, they'll know you're coming from a place of support and nurturing, and not anger or vindictiveness. A true friendship, a true relationship, is one in which you can have a conversation that's uncomfortable to have while knowing that you can have that conversation and move on and grow from it. Once again, it all comes back to being supported by strong foundations.

Money, and the relationship we have with it, is also something a lot of people struggle with. Money is a by-product of how well you do certain things in life, and if you build a solid foundation around your financial position and you invest correctly and spend wisely, you'll have a platform for your money to grow upon. The investment could be in anything—business, shares, property, or whatever type of investment suits you—but as long as you have built a solid enough relationship and that investment has a good base to grow upon, your money will grow and you can then reap the rewards as it starts to evolve and flourish.

Building the right foundations will support you in every transition you make through every stage of life, whether it's personal, family, health, or business related. You want to ensure that your transitions are solid enough to support you, so that you can continue to grow into the next stage. You can't do that if you don't have a solid foundation. If the foundations you've laid aren't strong enough, you're going to fall as you transition. It may not happen today, but at some point, without those foundations in place, you will certainly fall.

Your Life In Reflection

- It takes a solid foundation to ensure sustainability. Building the right foundations will support you in every transition you make through every stage of life, whether it's personal, family, health, or business related. When was the last time you checked what your foundations are like?

It's not what you do when people are watching that counts, it's what you do when you stay true to yourself and be what you were put on this earth to be and not trying to live someone else's life.

RALPH ANANIA

Chapter 14:

Be Authentic & Keep It Real

It's quite sad and unfortunate that we've become accustomed to living in a somewhat fake world, and society today has conditioned most people to believe they need to be someone they're not. When I started my keynote speaking journey back in 2010, I was new to the industry and felt I had to be somebody I wasn't. This doesn't mean that I wasn't presenting my true story, but the way I was presenting myself wasn't really me. I was always dressed in a suit and tie, and when I look back now, I feel I was rigid and not as playful as my natural self.

I was taught that you had to be a certain way, look a certain way, and show a certain side of yourself to people. In all honesty, maintaining this constructed appearance all the time becomes consuming and extremely tiring. You start to become someone you're not because you start to believe your own lies, and that right there is the problem we have in today's world. Authenticity is about being comfortable with your imperfect self. Just have a look at a mother and her new-born baby. It doesn't matter what anybody else thinks of that child, in the eyes of the mother, that baby is the most beautiful thing in the world. Why? Because it's real. The baby is beautiful because that's what God's creation has delivered. That's what life is about. Being comfortable with your imperfect self.

Authenticity is about staying true to what you *believe,* and *not* to your image. It's not about the way you look or how you put yourself out there on social platforms. That's the fake side of society. Social media is fantastic in a lot of ways, but it irks me when we start creating false impressions with all the filters and touch-up tools available to make us look 'better.' It may start off as a bit of fun, but those who have low self-esteem want to actually be like that, so you see people going to extremes just to make themselves look 'social media perfect.'

If those images are the way someone sees you, those images form their expectation, which won't hold true when they meet you face-to-face. It doesn't serve you when the impression someone has is not the impression they get when they meet you. I once met a regular follower of my video postings in a restaurant. It was the first time they'd met me in real life, and the first thing they said was, "Wow! You look exactly like you do in all your videos and pictures." I had to stop and think about why they'd say that, and I now realize why: there are a lot of people out there posting pictures of themselves that aren't really them, showing only the filtered and touched-up versions that present a different image.

When I first started out as a speaker, I used to see a lot of people hiding behind a podium or a slideshow presentation, and for a little while I was doing that too, but the reality is that this is also a mask. You shouldn't hide behind anything. Today (and since a long time now), I prefer to get off the stage and go down into the audience. I prefer to walk the floor, touching people's shoulders, connecting with them and making them feel that they're important to me and that I'm speaking to an individual and not just a room full of people. I'll speak to one person, putting my hand on their shoulder and looking them in the eye, and it doesn't matter if there's thousands of people in the room, I get off the stage and walk the floor to keep it real.

I want people to know and feel that I'm just like them, I'm no one special, and even though they'll come to me at the end of an event and make me feel like I'm a superstar, I know I'm not. At the end of the day, I'm just being myself and I've connected with them, and that's exactly what they feel. Yes, there are times when people put me on a pedestal, but if you let it get to your head, it can become quite dangerous.

I've seen a lot of speakers getting caught up in that, thinking they are better than everyone else. A lot of people get caught up in the importance of being famous, but the reality is they're living in a false world. I've experienced this first-hand all over the world with some great speakers: they'll come off stage and be greeted by a group of people that want to talk to them, and they'll think they're a superstar, but in the real world, when they walk out onto the street, no one even knows who they are.

Just be yourself and be true to the people you connect with, and that will shine through. There's so much that's fake in the speaking and presenting world. The amount of rubbish we get presented with really means nothing. What's important is showing someone that you've been in their shoes, been able to navigate through your journey under similar circumstances, and have come through it stronger, so that you can show them how to navigate through it because they might not know how to go about it. That's keeping it real. That's authenticity.

Putting up a picture in your presentation of you sitting on the bonnet of a sports car or in front of a mansion is meaningless, because anybody can put a picture up. The same applies to those who show a photo of themselves with a famous person, wanting you to believe that's who they 'hang out' with. This comes across as a desperate attempt to elevate their own presence. They're trying to make themselves look important because they have little or no substance in what they're delivering, so they've got to put themselves up on a pedestal to convince the audience that they're 'important.' This is just so wrong. It's fake, false and misleading, and nine times out of ten, if you tipped those people upside down, they wouldn't have two cents to rub together, and that's disappointing because they still manage to fool so many innocent people.

We're being conditioned in a lot of ways to look up to those with all these 'things' and to see them as great, but the reality is that they're not that great after all. I prefer to be real and to share my true-life stories of what I've achieved and how I've come through challenges. Anything I've had or accumulated throughout this time is irrelevant, it doesn't mean anything. What matters is letting people know I've been in their shoes, and that I can show them the path I took and therefore help them to get through the issues or challenges that they're currently facing in life.

Keeping it real is what makes life more enjoyable because it's effortless. Sure, there may be some challenges that you need to navigate through, but it's not *hard* work. Trying to be something or someone you're not means continually working at something that's not real—that's hard work. The authenticity part comes from you being comfortable in your own skin, being able to express your genuine feelings and personal views of life. By not being authentic, the only person you really fool is yourself, so why would you do that? I think it's important that you look at yourself in the mirror and get to like what you see, because that's your reality: that's true, and that's you.

Fame is where we often see the opposite of authenticity. When people become famous, they find they have to stop being themselves and instead create a fantasy of what someone else wants them to be. This is why we see so many famous people diving into depression and moving to addiction. After a while, they simply can't handle the fame, or being out there in the public eye and having their fans wanting to be like them. Everything about them and their life is the complete opposite of their authentic self.

There are a few things you need to take on board about authenticity that will help you find, and also make you comfortable in being, your true self:

First is to increase your self-awareness. Authenticity is not something you just have; it's something you pursue. It's part of learning. It's the painful part of your journey as a human being, but you need the learning experiences to develop self-awareness because without it, you're going to get caught and fall into the trap of being somebody that you're not. Social pressures are definitely a big factor, so you need to be clear on what you believe authenticity is and live by that.

Don't make any adjustments because of a comment or a suggestion made by someone who thinks they have a say in who you should be. It's a good idea to write down what you believe personal authenticity is, and then reflect on who you currently are and who you want to be. Most importantly, take away the lesson of who you *don't* want to be, because that will play a big part in showing you your true self and whether you want to be authentic or not.

Sometimes, when moving through life, we tend to put on or hide behind a façade. We get caught up in the act and that façade remains with us, like a mask covering our identity, a mask of whoever we're trying to be. Stop wearing that mask. If you've put it on throughout your life without realizing it, take the time to understand where and why you put it on. Find it and take it off, because it's not going to serve you anymore. It may work in certain workplaces and events where you need to uphold an image, but it won't work for long. You are who you are, and if people don't like you then that's their problem and not yours. Don't get caught up in the smoke and mirrors, and just be true to yourself.

Authenticity also means embracing vulnerability, so that you're not scared to be who you are and you don't get caught up in what people think. This is hard, because there are a lot of people who are concerned with what others think of them, and this is a flaw you need to be aware of. When you're authentic, it doesn't matter even when you make mistakes because genuine people accept mistakes. The fact that you've made one and it hasn't affected you is what keeping it real is all about. We all make mistakes, that's how we learn, but some people think they'll lose credibility by making a mistake. Not always. Credibility is lost when there's deception or deliberate misleading, not when you've made a mistake and you're being true to yourself and authentic.

The next thing to take on board is to just be present. One of the hardest things for people to do is to just be present, and not to have expectations or be judgmental. When you're with others and you're present, your authenticity becomes palpable, so you don't have to do anything. You don't have to show anyone that you're authentic; it will just happen naturally because that's who you are, so just be comfortable with being in your own skin.

Give yourself permission to be able to change and make the slight adjustments you need as you continue to navigate through life. As you adjust to the changes that happen in your life, your authenticity will automatically flow with that change. You need to be able to give yourself permission to change and not remain stuck being the person you believe you need to show people. If you're in the same place you were 20 years ago, you're not being true to yourself, and you're not being authentic. So, allow yourself to change. Give yourself permission that it's okay to accept that change.

Think inward but look outward. Authentic people are normally deep thinkers who generate a power by introspecting from within and then transpose that power outward, so the added value benefits others more than it does themselves. Think inward and then portray that outward to whoever you want to reach.

Authenticity plays a big part in how you treat people, how you speak to them, the ways you care for them, and doing it without any expectation is what authenticity is based upon. It's you just being yourself and giving to others rather than putting yourself above them. I am very conscious about never putting myself above anybody. I don't care how much money someone has or how well-educated they are, I never put myself below them either, because that doesn't make them a better person. Being better educated or having more money means nothing by itself.

We're all human beings, and we're all equal in that we've been put on this earth to achieve and deliver our pathway and purpose. Money and education don't make you a better person, but a lot of people get lost in that notion, thinking that what they have compared to someone else makes them a better person. I have more skills in business than many others, but that doesn't make me a better person. How you treat people is what is extremely important and what best characterises your true self.

It's also important to be fair, and to open up opportunities for those who may not see them. There are a lot of people out there who aren't as open-minded and therefore miss out on opportunities, which you can highlight and bring to their attention. One of the things about being authentic and real is that you're always open to new things and you always look for opportunities. Helping others become aware of the opportunities that are in front of them is all part of how you treat people and pass on a level of respect and kindness.

When you put up a façade, wear a mask, and try to be somebody you're not, it makes you unapproachable. Being accessible to everyone is something I've always been extremely careful about. Yes, I've been inundated by people after an event and they all want to share their story, and sometimes it can be a little overwhelming because you've got dozens of people waiting to speak to you and you can't speak to all of them, but you should always be approachable in some way, shape or form. Otherwise, it breeds arrogance, and you begin to develop the false belief that you're better than everyone else. So, as much as I can, I always make sure that I remain grounded and speak to anybody who wants to speak to me. Be approachable and it will shine through, and people will see you in a different light.

Your Life In Reflection

- Authenticity is about staying true to what you believe and *not* your image. Just be yourself and be true to the people you connect with, and that will shine through.
- By not being authentic, the only person you really fool is yourself. How does this play out in your life and is there any change required?

The more positive energy you create, the more it allows us to feel good about ourselves, and when you feel good about yourself everything else in your life flows.

RALPH ANANIA

Chapter 15:
Live Your Life
Without Limitations

L ife is a journey and moving into uncharted waters isn't always easy. There's an element of fear and anxiety that comes into play, which can make you quite uncomfortable. But the rewards that come from learning how to live your life without limitations will bring you a life filled with peace and fulfilment. You must, however, be prepared to move out of your comfort zone to be able to achieve this.

As I've mentioned a few times now, we live in a very materialistic world today where our values are governed by what we see. Yet, faith teaches us that we need to trust and believe what we can't see, and we will only see it once we believe it. When you connect to your spirit and focus internally, you discover so much about yourself that you didn't even realize was there. We are all born with the greatest gift on the planet, our mind, which is more capable than any super-computer ever built, yet most of us go through life without taking the time to discover its full potential. It's like driving a Ferrari but never taking it out of first gear; you know you have the power, you have total control, but you're too scared to open it up and see what this baby can really do.

If you want to achieve more and live more, you must accept this number one guiding principle: *when you live life on your terms, limits aren't real.*

When you play by everyone else's rules, then by default you're accepting their terms, boundaries and constraints. But here's the interesting part: you have complete control of yourself, therefore you have the freedom to choose how far you're prepared to go, how far you want to stretch and expand your mind. You get to decide whose game you're playing, yours or theirs. The challenge, on the other hand, is that even though we all have the ability to fly free, so to speak, many of us rarely move out of our comfort zone.

Now, if you truly desire to live a life free of limitations, you will need to overcome resistance from the following sources:

Let's start with *Your Mind:*

When you tell yourself things like *"I'm not good enough"* or *"I'm not qualified enough"* or *"I could never achieve anything like that,"* guess what? You never will, because what you're doing is limiting your potential. You've basically robbed yourself of life-enriching opportunities. In other words, you've just chosen to opt out.

Living life fully is about trying new things, even if you're not quite sure that they're going to work out. It's about the enjoyment gained from those moments that make it exciting, that allow you to explore what you may consider as your 'imperfect' self, just continue to learn as you go, and then grow from that learning. There is nothing wrong with being imperfect. If someone deems something imperfect, that's only their opinion and not the truth.

Having spent most of my entire life in the fresh produce industry, I was able to learn a lot from Mother Nature and her wonderful creations; yet as a society, we have done a great job complicating even that. Growing up and visiting farms with my dad from a young age taught me how all types of fresh produce is grown and how mother nature plays a huge part in how that fruit or vegetable turns out for us to consume. This became an ever-bigger part of my business operations later in life, as I not only got to deal with and visit farms that supplied us right across the country, but I also had the opportunity to visit farms in other countries as well.

And here's what amazes me: growing up I remember so clearly that everything had a season, and when that particular produce came into season, especially with all the summer fruit, you would really look forward to it, because in those days it was considered a treat. One of my favorite fruits is Nectarines, and when they were in the peak of the season you could smell them a mile away; they had such a wonderful aroma and were as sweet as sugar to eat. They didn't always look 'perfect'; in fact, the more 'imperfect' they looked the sweeter they were to eat. You see, most stone fruit varieties naturally have what is known as sugar spot, which is very much like the freckles on a kid's face, and the more prominent these spots were, the sweeter the fruit was. Naturally created by Mother Nature.

What then happened over the years is that our supermarket giants wanted farmers to look into sturdier varieties that would withstand the customers picking up and handling that fruit to eliminate bruising and ultimately reducing waste. Once they achieved that, the focus then moved to wanting fruit that was much more appealing to the human eye, something that looked 'perfect.' This continued to the point where today, there are over 800 varieties of Nectarines alone, and the same applies to most other stone fruit as well. But the problem with that is, while new varieties were being developed to look better and handle better, they started to lose out on tasting better, which is why today we have fruit that looks amazing but tastes like cardboard.

Why? Because 'someone' decided that they wanted perfect-looking fruit, but 'perfect' by whose standards? We are now starting to come full circle again, and we see some of these supermarket stores carrying a complete range of 'imperfect' products, because the amount of produce that was being wasted because it didn't fit the 'perfect' category was horrendous and costing millions of dollars to our poor farmers each year. No one knows better than Mother Nature and, in her eyes, everything she creates is in fact perfect.

Stop beating yourself up thinking you're imperfect because someone else has given you that label. If the stars always needed to be aligned for the universe to move forward, we wouldn't achieve much or get a great deal done. So instead of focusing on all the reasons why you shouldn't do something, make a list of all the reasons why you should, and you'll be amazed at how that will shift your perception of the situation completely.

Now let's look at *the advice and opinions of those closest to you:*

Most of the time, those closest to you only want what's best for you and will often try and shield you from what they may consider as a painful or uncomfortable situation. What generally happens is they encourage you to stay within certain 'boundaries.' But we never tend to ask, who actually established those boundaries and how will they serve us better? As I said, most of them really do mean well, but no matter how cautious you are, an unfortunate situation will find you at some point.

So instead of living in a bubble, why not go and explore what life is really about? Sure, you may find some bumps along the way, but the experience and opportunities it will bring far outweigh the bumps that you might endure on the journey. No one ever achieved greatness by being cautious; they created greatness because they were prepared to go where no one else had ever gone and were ready to deal with whatever challenges were thrown at them along the way. Don't let the opinions of others prohibit you from creating the greatness that is living inside of you. I **know** you can do it, but you have to 'believe' you can do it.

Living life with *Status Quo:*

If you get frustrated by the phrase *"because that's how it's always been done,"* then you will understand the danger that comes from accepting the status quo as a life sentence.

As I keep saying, society has conditioned us to accept what should and shouldn't be done, which is fine if you want to be amongst the mediocre. If not, then step up and challenge it.

On May 6, 1954, a young man, Roger Bannister, broke the record of running one mile in four minutes, a feat that had never been achieved. Many tried before Roger, but no one had ever been able to break the 4-minute mile, which Roger had run in 3:59.4 minutes. Then on June 21, 1954, just six weeks later, John Landy, a young Australian came out and ran the mile in 3:57.9 minutes.

Since then, over 1,500 athletes have run the mile under 4 minutes. If Roger Bannister had simply accepted the status quo of *it can't be done*, he would not have broken the record. In every situation where change or innovation or advancement is made, someone had to stand up and push through what others deemed impossible.

Moving into uncharted waters isn't always easy; there may be discomforts. But when you're able to push through the barriers of your limiting beliefs, you will find the rewards to be well and truly worth it. You will want to continue to explore and achieve so much more and be well on your way to living an extraordinary life. Just remember though, everything you want lies on the other side of fear. When you let go of the fear, the opportunities become abundant.

Your Life In Reflection

- If you want to achieve more and live more, you must accept this number one guiding principle: *when you live life on your terms, limits aren't real*. What limits have you put on yourself and how have they been serving you?

No matter what you're going through or where you are in life right now, there is a brighter future waiting for you. Just take a breath, reset and re-align, and learn to truly trust the process to bring you back on track to where you need to be.
RALPH ANANIA

Chapter 16:

Leave The Baggage Behind

've always loved listening to music. Growing up in the '70s and '80s, I enjoyed listening to American singer, Dionne Warwick—Whitney Houston's aunt, for those who don't know. Dionne Warwick released a Gold Record in 1979 for her hit single *I'll Never Love This Way Again*. At the time, I was in my teens and I just loved the song, not really taking any notice of the meaning behind the lyrics.

Recently, I came across the song again and as I was listening away, I reached the part of the song that says something about tomorrow slipping out of the hands of a supposed fool because he was thinking of yesterday. The reality of the lyrics dawned on me in that moment. And the reason I say this is that many times we find ourselves stuck because we continue holding on to our past, which then robs us of our future.

One of the most profound quotes I have ever heard is, "Let go and let God," which in itself requires you to take a huge leap of faith. However, you will never be able to move forward in life and achieve whatever it is that you want to achieve while you continue to carry the baggage of your past with you. Your past does not equal your future; what got you to where you are will not necessarily get you to where you want to be. Yes, sometimes we do need to trust the process and just let God or the Universe take care of it.

After my separation, I spent the best part of three years working on myself where I had to face my past head-on and go through some very painful processes. At the time, I could not for the life of me see the light at the end of the tunnel. However, this pushed me way out of my comfort zone, allowed me to grow and made me see that I would never move forward and live my true purpose if I continued to carry the baggage of my past around with me. The incredible thing is that once I realized it would no longer serve me and I completely detached myself from all of the past *limiting* beliefs I had, everything started to become crystal clear.

Now, just to give you an idea of where I was at, there were days, weeks and months when I struggled from one minute to the next. My life was completely and utterly turned upside-down. No matter what anyone told me at the time, I could not see past the next hour, let alone the next day. Here I was, someone who had overcome so many challenges in business over the years and built some successful organizations, who had presented on stage alongside some of the greatest thought leaders of our time, who had delivered programs to thousands of people right across the globe and completely changed people's lives, and yet I had come to a point where I couldn't function from one hour to the next. So believe me when I say this: once I came to that point where

I completely detached myself from all the baggage, everything started to fall into place.

There are many contributing factors that played a part in my healing, but the one thing that was consistent all the way through was the strength I drew from my children. They too were hurting, yet without any words required, the four of us together just knew what each of us needed to get through that dark time. They knew I was there for them no matter what, and I knew they were there for me no matter what. The bond that then formed became so strong that it can never be broken, because together and as a family, we all weathered the biggest storm of our lives.

No one enjoys suffering. But in the hands of God, trials become tools. He uses hardship to shape us into the person He wants us to be, because He has bigger plans for us. There are many moments when I've sat back and reflected on where I tended to ignore the signs, and it's amazing how quickly you realize that when your spirit is awake, you are very alert to everything that is happening around you.

The markers are always there, but if you're not aware and alert and in tune with your spirit, you will always miss them. One of the most important lessons I learnt in this time was not to ignore the signs when they appeared. Always try to understand what they mean and what you must change or reconsider before moving forward.

Once you allow yourself to heal, you will be able to see things from a different perspective. You'll be able to allow people into your life again and to receive love again. When you're ready to receive again, regardless of how that looks for you, you'll be amazed at the doors that God opens up for you. There are those who expect God to wave a magic wand and give them whatever it is that they're asking for, but it doesn't happen that way. What 'we' think we want is not necessarily in line with what God's bigger plans are. Therefore, He protects us from ourselves, so we don't go down the wrong path 'again.'

So, no matter what storm you are facing right now, always remember that it will pass. After a harsh winter comes a beautiful spring, after rain comes sunshine, after the dark of the night comes daylight. Your storm will pass, but you must not fight it; otherwise, it will take a great deal longer for you to get through it. As I've said before, my faith is what pulled me through some of the darkest hours of my life. Regardless of the religious or spiritual beliefs you may have, if you keep the faith, you will also be able to run the race and build a bigger and brighter future, not only for yourself but more importantly for those closest to you.

Some of the tools that I still use today are:

To stand on God's promises. It's amazing what strength you can gain from scripture in tough times. They say the Bible is the greatest book of all times and it is so true. One of the most powerful stories for me is the book of Job. If you haven't read it, do yourself a favor and read it, because as much as it's filled with tragedy and sadness, it also has so much inspiration to draw from.

Don't ever stop Praying. Prayer is a conversation with God, whether you're in the car driving or having a shower; you don't need to be in a church to pray. I pray before I walk into a meeting, just asking for God's protection.

Don't hide your faith. Be proud and stand tall. You don't have to flaunt your belief in God, but you don't need to hide it either. There have been many a conversation where I openly speak about my personal journey and how my faith in God has got me through some tough years, and more times than not, the person I'm speaking with will take much encouragement from our conversation. Now I'm not preaching the Bible to them and I'm very clear—that's not my calling. I'm merely sharing my own personal experience with my faith and how it got me through some of the most challenging times of my life. There's a big difference!

There's a great movie called *Facing the Giants* which is about a Christian high school football coach. If you haven't seen it, do yourself a favor and watch it asap, for you will draw so much from it. There's one particular part in the movie where the coach is really struggling and the school pastor walks right into his office with the Bible open and just starts reading:

"Revelation Chapter 3 says: We serve a God that opens doors that no one can shut, and he shuts doors that no one can open."

"He Says: Behold, I have placed before you an open door that no one can shut. I know you have little strength, yet you have kept my word and have not denied my name."

He then closes the Bible and says:

"Coach Taylor, the Lord is not through with you yet. You still have an open door here, and until the Lord moves you, you're to bloom right where you're planted. I just felt led to come and tell you that today." And then he proceeds to walk out of Coach Taylor's office.

Coach Taylor then gets up from behind his desk and follows him into the hallway and says:

"Mr. Bridges, do you believe God told you to tell me that? I admit to you that I have been struggling. But I've also been praying, I just don't see Him at work here."

Mr. Bridges then says:

"Grant, I heard a story about two farmers who desperately needed rain. And both of them prayed for rain, but only one of them went out and prepared his fields to receive it. Which one do you think trusted God to send the rain?"

Grant replies with: *"The one who prepared his fields for it."*

Mr. Bridges then says: *"Which one are you? God will send the rain when He's ready. You need to prepare your field to receive it."*

Learn to trust the process and Believe. Believe in yourself, believe that you will get through your storm and believe that when you ask you will receive. You also need to be open and ready to receive it though!

When you continually focus on the past, you will never be prepared to receive the abundance that's meant for you in the future. It may not always look the way you want it to, but it's only when you stop hanging on to the past, see through the mess and find the message, that you will get through your storm; you will always achieve the outcome you truly deserve.

Your Life In Reflection

- You will never be able to move forward in life and achieve whatever it is that you want to achieve while you continue to carry the baggage of your past around with you. What baggage do you need to get rid of in your life right now to move forward and live the life you deserve?

When life throws you a challenge and you look hard enough, there is always a lesson to be learnt. Find the lesson, be grateful for the experience, move forward and never stop learning.

RALPH ANANIA

Chapter 17:

Learn From Real-life Experiences

H ave you ever looked back at some point in your past and thought, I wish I had learnt that lesson a long time ago?

Life in general is a continuous learning process and, more often than not, we need to experience life to gain the lesson. It seems that 'life lessons' are called that for a reason. The more life you experience, the more lessons you accumulate and the more powerful those lessons become. Some of those extremely valuable lessons can be learnt from wise thinkers and experts as well as from friends and family.

Although some lessons must be learnt through experience, you don't have to wait until you're old to become aware of what's truly meaningful and worthwhile. You simply need the curiosity and desire for self-awareness and personal growth. Once you learn the lesson, you can apply it in your life at any age and enjoy the benefits that enhance your happiness and well-being. In other words, you're never too old to learn, and you should never close your mind to learning whatever your age or circumstances are.

Then we have the lessons that we must learn the hard way, which I'm sure most can relate to. Those lessons usually come at a cost, be it financial or personal. This happens when we let our pride and ego get in the way, but these lessons can also be the most powerful ones you will ever learn if you are willing to open your mind and grow from the experience.

An open mind lets you accomplish so much from life's experiences, making them the greatest motivators in realizing your goals and reaching your destination. There's a whole other book that can be written on my own life lessons, but here's the thing: what life teaches us cannot be learnt from a textbook at university. What's important to understand, though, is how powerful these lessons become when you apply them as you continue to move forward through life.

Here are just some of the lessons I've learnt which may help you on your journey and even highlight some areas that you may have neglected.

Look after your health and wellbeing, for this is the key to everything you do. If you're anything like me, you must have thought you're invincible in your younger years and taken your health for granted. It's not until much later in life when you're a lot older that you start to reflect and make the necessary changes to preserve your health and wellbeing as much as possible.

Create your own path and live your life. There is a genius in all of us, but you will never allow that genius to come out if you are living someone else's life. Don't let the pressure of others determine your destination. Stay true to yourself and shine just as you were meant to shine, regardless of what that looks like for you. On the same token, don't judge others because of what we've been told or made to believe, as more often than not, those people have their own underlying issues to deal with and are looking externally to justify their own mistakes.

Value time. Life is a speeding bullet, and the older you get the faster time seems to fly. Make the most of each day and leave your mark and appreciate the journey so you don't have regrets.

Be grateful for what you have. The more grateful we are, the more positive energy we create, and the better we feel about ourselves, which makes everything in your life flow smoothly. Take some time and write a list of all the things you're grateful for and see how you feel afterwards. You'll be surprised.

Choose kindness every time. Acts of kindness bring people together, which also makes you feel good about yourself. When you are kind, others are kind to you. There is too much bitterness, anger and negativity in the world, so choose to be different and rise above all the doom and gloom. Put a smile on someone else's face and watch your world shine.

Don't be scared to push the boundaries because of your own limiting beliefs. If you don't take risks, you won't grow. Most people never move forward because someone has told them that it's 'too risky.' Again, most times, the person saying that is too scared to even mitigate that risk, which is why they stop you from taking action. If you try something and fail at it, take the lesson and try again; but you will never gain the lesson if you don't even try. To achieve real growth, you must move out of your comfort zone.

Open your heart and don't be afraid to be vulnerable. Express your feelings and show your true spiritual self to others. If they judge you for that then you don't need them in your life. Sometimes we just have to make that call.

Let go of your past. Forgive those you need to forgive and don't hold on to any anger as it will only stop you from moving forward. Rejection will come at some point in your life, deal with it as you wish, but the sooner you accept it and handle it with grace, the better you'll be.

Stay humble and take care of those who matter most. Don't ignore those closest to you as they will always be there for you regardless of what's happening around you.

Be yourself. We are all born with a unique DNA; this in itself tells us that we are different to everyone else and distinct in our own way, so just be yourself and embrace your uniqueness and watch it shine.

Never give up. Regardless of how hard things get, keep pushing through and you will never stop learning.

There's a story from many years ago that tells of an elementary school teacher whose name was Mrs. Thompson. As she stood in front of her fifth-grade class on the first day of school, she told her children a lie. Like most teachers, she looked at her students and told them that she loved them all the same. But that simply was not true, because there in the front row, slumped in his seat, was a little boy named Teddy Stoddard.

Mrs. Thompson had watched Teddy the year before and noticed that he didn't play well with the other children. His clothes were messy and he was constantly in need of a bath. Teddy could be unpleasant at times. It got to the point where

Mrs. Thompson would take delight in marking his papers with a broad red pen and making bold 'X's and finally putting a big 'F' on the top.

At the school where Mrs. Thompson taught, she was required to review each child's past records. She put Teddy's off till last. When she finally reviewed his file, she was in for a surprise. Teddy's first-grade teacher had written, "Teddy is a bright child with a ready laugh. He does his work neatly and has good manners. He's a joy to be around." His second-grade teacher had written, "Teddy is an excellent student and well-liked by his classmates, but he's troubled because his mother has a terminal illness and life at home must be a struggle." His third-grade teacher had written, "His mother's death has been hard on him. He tries to do his best, but his father doesn't show much interest. His home life will soon affect him if steps aren't taken." Teddy's fourth-grade teacher had written, "Teddy is withdrawn and doesn't show much interest in school. He doesn't have many friends and sometimes he even sleeps in class."

By now, Mrs. Thompson realized the problem and was ashamed of herself. She felt even worse when her students brought her Christmas presents wrapped in beautiful ribbons and bright paper—except Teddy, whose present was clumsily wrapped in heavy brown paper that he got from a grocery bag. Mrs. Thompson took pains to open it in the middle of the other presents. Some of the children started to laugh when she pulled out a rhinestone bracelet with some of the stones missing and a bottle that was one quarter full of perfume.

But she stifled the children's laughter when she explained how pretty the bracelet was while putting it on and then dabbing some of the perfume on her wrist. Teddy Stoddard stayed after school that day just long enough to say, "Mrs. Thompson, today you smell just like my mom used to." After the children left, she cried for at least an hour.

On this very day, she quit teaching reading, writing and arithmetic and instead began to teach children. Mrs. Thompson began to pay close attention to Teddy as she worked with him. As time went on his mind seemed to come alive. The more she encouraged him, the faster he responded. By the end of the year, Teddy had become one of the smartest children in the class. Despite her lie, he had become one of her darling pets. A year later, she found a note under the door from Teddy telling her that she was the best teacher he had ever had in his whole life.

Six years passed by and to her surprise, another note came from Teddy. He wrote that he had finished high school third in his class and that she was still the best teacher he had ever had in his whole life. Four years later another letter came, saying that while things had been tough at times, he had stayed in school and stuck with it and that he had graduated from college with the highest of honors. He assured Mrs. Thompson that she was still the very best and favorite teacher he had ever had in his whole life.

Four more years passed by and yet another letter came. This time he explained that after he got his bachelor's degree, he had decided to go a little further. Again, he assured her that she was still his best and most-loved teacher. The letter this time was signed Theodore F. Stoddard, MD.

The story doesn't end there. There was one final letter that spring. Teddy said that he had met this girl and that he was going to be married. He explained that his father had died a couple years earlier and he was wondering if Mrs. Thompson might agree to sit in the place, at his wedding, that was usually reserved for the mother of the groom. Of course, Mrs. Thompson did. She wore that bracelet, the one with several rhinestones missing.

She also made sure she was wearing the perfume that Teddy remembered his mother wearing on their last Christmas together. After the wedding, they hugged each other as Dr. Stoddard whispered in Mrs. Thompson's ear, "Thank you so much for making me feel important and showing me that I could make a difference." Mrs. Thompson, with tears in her eyes, whispered back, "Teddy, you have it all wrong. You were the one who taught me that I could make a difference. I didn't know how to teach until I met you."

I first heard Dr. Wayne Dyer tell this story many years ago and have heard it again many times since, still it brings tears to my eyes every single time. As I often reflect over the years of my life, there were times when I too, like Mrs. Thompson, had judged someone by their appearance without ever considering what they may have been going through. We all go through life with our own challenges, good, bad or indifferent, and we all share them at some point. Showing kindness costs us nothing, yet delivers so much to the one receiving it.

So, the next time you find yourself in a situation where you're about to pass judgment, regardless of that person's race, color, religion or gender, just stop for a moment and think about what else may be going on in their life and how a simple smile may make a huge difference to their day. And if you look hard enough, there will always be a lesson for you to take away and learn from that experience.

Your Life In Reflection

- What life teaches us cannot be learnt from a textbook at university. What's important to understand is how incredibly powerful these lessons become when you apply them as you continue to move forward through life. What can you take away from those life lessons that you can easily implement into your life right now?

When the student is ready, the teacher will appear.—Ancient Proverb

RALPH ANANIA

Where to from here —in Conclusion

What is my purpose? This is by far one of the most common questions I get asked.

The real purpose of life is happiness. This means finding joy in everything you do, not finding happiness in everything you've accumulated. Most people tend to go through life without knowing where their destination is, and therefore they never arrive there. You'll find your purpose when you're able to connect to your spiritual self and shift your focus from your head to your heart. It's the spirit that gives you life, but your head is always looking for control, so you tend to become confused as to what your purpose in life really is.

So, no matter where you are in your life right now, use this time to sit back and reflect. Take note of where you've come from and, more importantly, what you've come through, and then reassess because the world has changed from what we knew, and it will continue to change for some time. The process of reflecting and reassessing will allow you to grow and evolve.

As I look back on my journey, there have been many times where I've had to stop, reflect and reassess to stay on track and continue moving forward. And what I'm going to share with you here is what helped me navigate through some of those challenging times, which allowed me to get to where I am today. They will hopefully also help you on your journey towards understanding where it is that you truly want to get to.

Take the time to define your own path.

You're never going to be able to control someone else's actions, but you absolutely *can* control your own actions. You don't want to react/respond to or manifest life minute by minute, you want to get comfortable with always taking the higher road. When you take that higher road, life gets much better. You're able to define your own path and live the journey the way you believe you want to see it through, not necessarily the way someone else wants you to or thinks you should.

Remember to keep looking in the mirror.

What I mean by that is, whatever you put out in life is what will come back. It's a direct reflection of your actions. There's enough negativity in the world already, and we don't want to be consumed by it, so it's important to remember there are many positives out there too and to move your focus towards them. There are many wonderful people in the world who really go out of their way to take care of others, people who take care of one another, and through every crisis or pandemic, there will always be those who will go over and above to take care of someone else.

This is why you must always remember to look in the mirror, because what we see and hear in the media is not what we need to believe all the time. We should do what we believe God has given us as our purpose, to help those around us and to move forward. It's not just about the money or material things; it's about doing something because you want to do it and enjoy doing it. When you open up your heart and do things from a place of love, whether it's giving or helping, the world will look much different and become a much better place for everyone.

Show everyone around you what's on the inside.

It's not what you look like externally that's going to make a difference in the world, it's what you put out from inside yourself; that's what's important and that's what you want to show the world. Genuine people see right through what's on the outside, and with the world continually changing as fast as it is, everyone is alert and will know when you're putting it on.

By showing the world what's on the inside, you'll start to enjoy life a whole lot more. You'll have less stress, you won't be as disappointed, you won't be as frustrated, and you won't need to prove anything to anyone. Your inner peace, compassion and love will shine through, and you'll find patience. Even when things get tough, you'll be able to deal with it and handle it a lot better. That's your true self, that's your core, and there's no need to hide that.

Take a good look at where you've been fishing.

Take a good look at where you've been fishing as you may need to fish from another pond. What I mean by this is that you need to surround yourself with the right people. We can't always choose our family but we can always choose our friends, so make the commitment to surround yourself with people who are going to encourage you and have your back when you need it, people you can trust and can confide in, and people who aren't going to take advantage of your goodness.

Surrounding yourself with the right people allows you to flourish. You want people around you who are going to challenge and stretch your boundaries because they want to make sure you're growing, even if that tough love is sometimes hard to take. But you definitely don't want to surround yourself with people who continually question everything you do and put you down or make you feel small or belittle you. You may not have realized that this has been happening up until this point, but you need to look closely at the people you're surrounding yourself with. It may be time to do a little bit of spring-cleaning in your closet of friends.

Get comfortable being your authentic self.

A lot of people are uncomfortable with just being themselves, because they believe they need to be someone else. They believe they need to show the world someone better than the person they really are, but that couldn't be further from the truth. All you need to be is the person you were put on this earth to be. Being who you believe you should be is what being comfortable with your authentic self is about. You don't need to turn into a recluse or an introvert; you just need to be your authentic self and drop all façades.

Sometimes it may seem that you're in a lonely place, but this is only because you're going through the transition. If you can really understand your authentic self and fall in love with that person, it will absolutely shine through everything you do. Once you truly become comfortable with yourself, everyone else around you will feel it. This will then also help you get through any challenging times that arise, because you can actually push through all of the noise and get straight to the core of where you want to be.

Have fun along the way and enjoy the ride.

We often spend a lot of time doing things we believe will get us to the place we eventually want to get to, but we don't have any fun along the way. So by the time we get there, we'll sit back and question, "Was it really all worth it?" One area where such thoughts are very common concerns children. Most of the successful people I've had the opportunity to work with and associate with spend their entire life working so hard to build something for their children, that they actually forget to enjoy their children along the way.

When the time comes and they've built what they wanted to build, their children have grown and don't want any part of them because they're living their own life. I've had many a conversation where they say, "I've worked my entire life to ensure the kids are financially secure, and now they're doing their own thing and don't even appreciate what I've done for them." Maybe that is the case, maybe their children don't appreciate what they've done, but they need to find a balance between building for the future *and* enjoying it along the way. The time that you miss with your children today will never come back, so have fun along the way and enjoy the ride, whatever that looks like for you. Whether you have children or not, take time out for yourself and those closest to you.

Control your thoughts and set yourself achievable expectations.

You can expect great things from life, but you need to control your thoughts. Many times at different stages in life, you might be confronted with that little voice in your head that tells you *'you're not good enough'* or *'you can't do it'* or *'you don't have the skillset'* or *'you'll never amount to anything.'* All those little nuggets of self-doubt must be put to the side. Learn to control those thoughts, maybe by thanking them when they arrive. "Thank you for sharing, now move on, because I'm actually going to achieve what I've set out to achieve."

Those voices don't serve you. Those voices are not you, those voices are doubt, and you don't want to be caught up in doubt. Set expectations that you know you can achieve, because too many people set expectations they can never achieve and therefore are always faced with disappointment. If you set expectations that you know you can achieve, then disappointment will no longer be there. This not only applies to yourself but also to the people around you. It's no good setting expectations for someone that you know they can't deliver, because then every time you look at that person, you're going to be faced with disappointment.

Don't allow the voice in your head to tell you what you can and can't do, and make sure you set expectations you can achieve so that you can continue to move forward. As we grow, we can set bigger expectations because we are then growing with our expectations. Setting expectations that you can't achieve is not growth, it's disappointment. The more real expectations you set for yourself, the more you'll be able to achieve them and the more you will grow and achieve great things from them.

Get inspired.

Dr. Wayne Dyer often said that inspire means 'in spirit' and when you work from your spirit, everything you do comes into alignment and you just flow. We all have our own spirit, an internal spiritual base. When you're working from that, your actions come from your core and everything flows effortlessly. We often see some people who we consider to be 'naturals' at what they do, but it's coming naturally to them because they're working and living from their spirit. When they're doing something that seems to be natural, it's usually because we see it being done almost effortlessly; it's who they're meant to be and it's what they're meant to be doing.

We are all born with a purpose, but most of us spend our lives looking and searching for what that purpose is. The reality is that we keep suppressing what we're meant to let out, because the world tells us or conditions us to be a certain way, behave a certain way, do something a certain way, and be someone we're not meant to be. We're told that this is how we need to be.

Inspiration keeps you motivated, and motivation is a huge part of growth and moving forward. We all need some form of motivation in life, but it's also important to simply understand and just be with yourself, to take the time to stop 'thinking' and just 'feel' what it is that you want to put out into the world. Be okay with that, whatever that looks like for you. Don't try to be someone else. Take the time to really connect with what inspires you, because that's how you will grow, evolve and flourish.

Leave a legacy.

Leaving a legacy is not about leaving money or possessions behind when you're gone, and it's not about having a building, or a street named after you. Leaving a legacy is about being more than a statistic and doing more than just fulfilling a role. We're born into this world to play our part in the growth and evolution of the next generation, and that's what life is about. Leaving a legacy is about leaving something for the next generation to continue with and build upon.

Regardless of whether you have children or not, leaving a legacy means fulfilling your purpose on this earth and allowing what you've created from that purpose to continue long after you're gone. My father was a very humble man who worked hard for most of his life to provide the best he could for his family.

He didn't set out with any grand plan of leaving a legacy for his children, but it happened anyway over a long period of time because he was fulfilling his purpose of making a difference towards the next generation. I wouldn't be the person I am if it wasn't for my father, and also my mother as a matter of fact. It's the 'ripple of influence' from inspired individuals who inspire others... We see it in sport all the time: coaches, athletes, next generation of athletes.

Your time on this earth is limited, so don't live someone else's life. Live by your dreams, your vision and your passion.

You now have the tools to let go of all your fears and limiting beliefs and to create the future that the world awaits from you.

I pray that the inspiration gained from reading this book will give you hope and fulfilment in everything you do.

Just keep moving forward and don't ever give up!

Your Life In Reflection

- Leaving a legacy is not about leaving money or possessions behind when you're gone, and it's not about having a building or a street named after you. Leaving a legacy is about being more than a statistic and doing more than just fulfilling a role. What legacy would you like to leave on this earth?

Acknowledgments

One of the greatest lessons of life is learning to be humble and appreciating those who have played a role in allowing you to grow and become the person you are today. I have been blessed to be connected with so many wonderful people who have been such an influence in my life, and this book wouldn't carry the same weight if it wasn't for the role each and every one of them played.

So, it is with deep gratitude that I express my appreciation to the following for their contributions.

First and foremost, to the God and father of us all, for His unwavering love and continual guidance in allowing me to pursue my journey in making a difference to as many souls as possible. To all my readers, thank you!

To the thousands of people in various settings right across the globe, who have trusted me to share my experience and teachings with you.

To my amazing clients, each and every one of you have made an impact in my life. Working with you has allowed me to continually grow and evolve into the person I am, and it wouldn't have been possible without sharing the journey and experience with you.

To Emily Gowor for your encouragement and belief in me all those years ago, that the world needed to be inspired by the wisdom I had to share. I am truly humbled to be here many years later with the finished product and have Emily and the Gowor International Publishing team bring this book to life.

To my very dear friend Jess Hartono, who believed in me and kept pushing me to get this book finished. And to Lina Purves, who was able to make some of the magic happen with her amazing guidance and support, I couldn't have finished it without you.

Thank you to my amazing friends for your continual support, for being there throughout my entire journey—the highs, the lows, the good and the not-so-good times—never once passing judgment and always supporting me in every aspect.

To my many amazing coaches:

Tony Robbins, who changed my life forever. Keith Cunningham, for the wisdom and knowledge he instilled in me many years ago. To the man who taught me how to "let go and let God"—the late Wayne Dyer who I adored and learnt so many wonderful lessons from.

To Kane Minkus, a man who is so much more than a friend. He showed me how to deliver my message and change the lives of many individuals across the globe.

To Jennifer Leone, the woman behind the presentations. I wouldn't be the speaker and presenter I am today if it wasn't for the invaluable lessons learnt from Jennifer.

To Melita Misoni, who showed me how to rebuild from the inside out, bring everything back to the core and allow my spirit to guide me on this journey.

To my family, while you may not have realized, you have all played a huge role in my life, to which I am forever grateful.

To my very dear friend Mahir Thaker, you played such an inspirational role in my life. You were always there when I needed to vent and would always give me your deepest spiritual insights. Your words are always with me and even though I miss you dearly I am blessed to have shared many wonderful moments with you that still put a smile on my face.

To Dev Singh, not only for your photography skills, but also for highlighting what I may have been missing and for always putting things into perspective for me.

To Harry Koutsos, words can't express the love and respect I have for you. A true friend in every aspect, always there with unfailing support regardless of the circumstances.

To Mum and Dad, who I miss dearly. The role your parents play is often not fully appreciated until they're gone. Words cannot express my love and appreciation for the sacrifices you made to allow me to become the person I am today. I know you are supporting and guiding me every day from heaven, and I owe you a debt of gratitude that can't be measured.

To my wonderful children: Michaela, Alexandra, and Christopher, you fill my heart with more joy than I can ever express. Your strength has allowed me to continually push forward, even when I thought I had nothing left. You are such an inspiration, and I couldn't be the person I am today if it wasn't for the love and support you continually give.

And finally, the love of my life, soul mate and best friend Carla Bastone, you truly are one of the most beautiful souls that God has ever put breath into. I wouldn't be the person I am today if it wasn't for the unconditional love and support you continually give.

About The Author

With over 35 years of business experience, an Australian Entrepreneur Award winner, International Keynote Speaker and Author, Ralph Anania is regarded as an authority in business transformation. Ralph has an impressive track record where he has successfully transformed 31 companies of his own into highly efficient enterprises, one of which exceeds $130 million in annual revenue, enabling him to share real business experience with thousands of clients in a variety of industries across the globe.

With his ability to turn ordinary businesses into finely tuned profitable enterprises and having raised over $500M in capital for various business acquisitions, Ralph is always in high demand. His credible business knowledge and expertise see him constantly play an important role, mentoring entrepreneurs who are focused on scaling their business and improving their strategy development to increase their company's bottom line.

As a seasoned International Keynote Speaker, Ralph has shared the stage with some of the greatest thought leaders of our time, where he delivers his real-life experience in such a practical way that everyone is engaged from the minute he steps out on stage, transforming millions of lives in the process.

Ralph has a number of programs that he has specifically created to transform your business and, more importantly, your life:

- Boost Your Business
- Master Your Business
- 8 Steps to 8 Figures
- Transform Your Life in 21 Days

Ralph also works privately with individuals who are looking for massive change through his one-on-one coaching.

TO BOOK RALPH FOR A KEYNOTE
OR SPEAKING PRESENTATION

LOG ONTO www.RalphAnania.com

A free ebook edition is available with the purchase of this book.

To claim your free ebook edition:

1. Visit MorganJamesBOGO.com
2. Sign your name CLEARLY in the space
3. Complete the form and submit a photo of the entire copyright page
4. You or your friend can download the ebook to your preferred device

Print & Digital Together Forever.

Snap a photo

Free ebook

Read anywhere

CPSIA information can be obtained
at www.ICGtesting.com
Printed in the USA
JSHW021301130622
27015JS00001B/44

9 781631 957987